Published by
Invincible Publishers

Published by

Invincible Publishers

201A, SAS Tower, Sector 38, Gurugram - 122003

Phone: +91-124-4034247, +91 9355675555

www.i-publish.in

This book is a work of fiction. Names, characters, places and incidents are either the product of the author's imagination or are used fictitiously. Any resemblance to real persons, living or dead, or actual events or locations, is purely coincidental and the publisher does not hold responsibility for the same.

First Published in 2020

ISBN: 978-93-89600-58-2

Dedicated to

'Everyone who has a heart that bleeds and eyes that weep.'

Contents

Acknowledgments

I am grateful to 'Invincible Publishers' for publishing my first collection of English poetry.

I want to express my gratitude to Mr. Swapan Seth for reviewing the poems and sharing his insights.

I want to offer special thanks to my sister Shruti Singh for the magnificent cover design and thoughtful illustrations. ***(www.shrutillusion.com)***

I want to thank my parents for not restraining me from going astray many times in my life.

I want to thank my friends for making me fall in love with my enemies.

I want to thank all my former girlfriends for stabbing me in the heart.

Preface

I do not know where to start.

But I know where to end.

Thus, I end it here.

Who can discern why one does what one does? Probably one does what one does out of love for that particular thing. In my case, I have a penchant for poetry. But more than poetry, it is the words that fascinate me. I abhor words as much as I adore them.

As far as motivation and inspiration are concerned, well, some people think and feel a lot. I am one of them, though what I think and feel is subjective and encircles my existence.

I detest categorizing feelings and emotions. Although you can glimpse by the title of the book that 'death' is a reccurring motif in my poetry, I don't feel compelled to elaborate upon it. I leave it on you all to figure that out.

If you are reading this preface, then I presume that you have the book in some form. You can go through the poems and see if you like them. There are very few things in life which we love and appreciate. If you like them, then possibly it will open a channel of communication between us in the future.

I am easily accessible, but you won't find me in an office or an event. You might find me in a cheap bar, drinking with strangers or on the roundabouts smoking a cigarette. It all depends!

You can surely find me on my terrace at night, but visit if you are up for a glass of wine, some cigarettes, and tearful talks.

Laudeep Singh

I myself am hell;
nobody's here.

- Robert Lowell

I shut my eyes and all the world drops dead; I lift my eyes and all is born again.

- Sylvia Plath

This world is gradually becoming a place where I do not care to be any more.

- John Berryman

Live or die, but don't poison everything.

- Anne Sexton

It isn't enough for your heart to break because everybody's heart is broken now.

- Allen Ginsberg

In darkness and in hedges
I sang my sour tone
and all my love was howling
conspicuously alone.

- W. D. Snodgrass

Conked out

Broken dreams
bear a resemblance
to underfed
malnourished babies,
vouching out of hunger,
unheeded by the parents,
left at a tender age
in the fare of life -
only to die
a plodding death
in the lap of time.

Flux

Life
is the practice ground
for telling a lie -
a beautiful lie
and death
is the preparation
for living the truth -
a hideous truth.

The skill,
however,
lies in converting
one into the other,
that is to say,
converting a beautiful lie
into a hideous truth
and converting a hideous truth
into a beautiful lie.

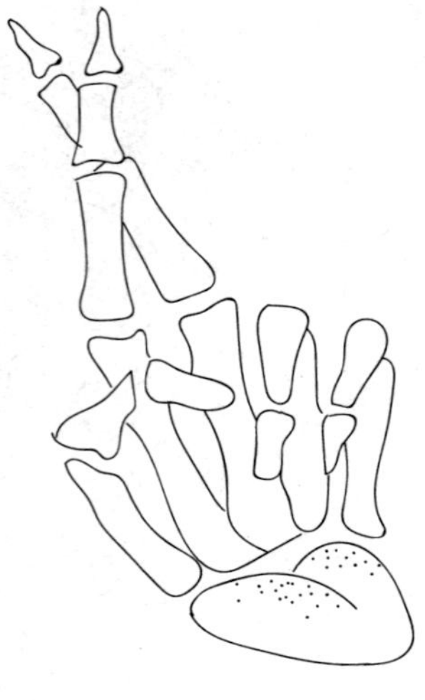

The seers of the world

Those who are born blind
can glimpse that
which is not discernible
to the physical eye;
for those
who can see
make sense
of this world
through an understanding
of binary opposites
but for those
who are born blind -
all dualities
cease to exist,
nothing makes sense to them
yet everything does
and as they grow,
in their heart grows
an innate sense of being.

Insanity

Sometimes
I wake up
in the middle of the night
to natter with the stars,
a kind of madness perhaps!

I ask the question
and I myself respond.

I myself snoop
and I myself howl.

The moon looks down upon me
akin to a Freudian spy
who is oblivious of the subtleties
that human beings go by
each year,
each month,
each day,
each hour,
each minute,
and each second
of their lives.

Purgatory

The demise
of a loved one
teaches
us everything
that is worth knowing
in this existence.

The only thing
that matters
is that whether
we yearn
to discover about it
on our own
or whether
we prefer
to be educated
about the same
by other individuals.

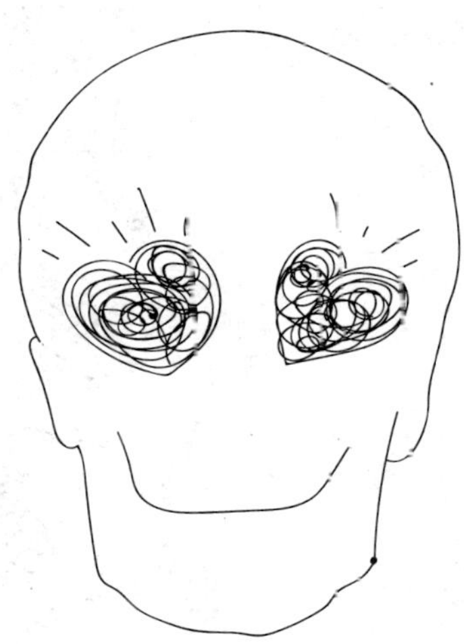

Time out

Wasted years,
wasted months,
and wasted days.

Wasting hours,
wasting minutes,
and wasting seconds.

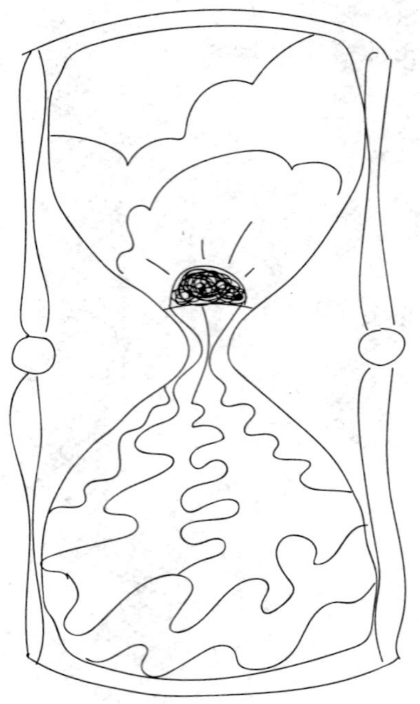

Nowhere to be found

When you gaze
into my eyes
and I gaze
into your eyes,
the 'you' disappears
and the 'I' disappears.

What remains
is untainted love,
wholesome consciousness,
and unblemished witnessing.

Show me the way

By what means
or arrangement
should I draw closer to you
that you become
enamoured by my love?

From which garden
which flower
should I get
that you become
enamoured by my love?

From which sea-shore
should I holler out your name
that you become
enamoured by my love?

Amongst
your other lovers,
whom should I impersonate
that you become
enamoured by my love?

By what kind of poise
should I propose my plea
that you become
enamoured by my love?

From which galaxy
which star
should I carry
that you become
enamoured by my love?

Which poet's verse
should I declaim
that you become
enamoured by my love?

From which ocean
which pearl
should I fetch
that you become
enamoured by my love?

If I draw closer to you
in the disguise of a tramp
with a beseeching bowl
in my hands,
will you become
enamoured by my love?

O beloved
of rosy countenance,
the treasure of my heart
and soul,
what should I utter
and what I shouldn't,

how should I act
and how I shouldn't,
via what means
or arrangement
should I draw closer to you
that you become
enamoured by my love?

The curse of memory

That evening,
which regrettably
was our last evening together
left an indelible dent
on my heart.

In the deepest recesses
of my breath,
the traces of your sweat
can still be found
and they become fragrant
with the slightest
thought of you,
brought in
by the blight of reminiscence.

The last time we met,
the black eyeliner
which suited you preeminently
trickled down your cheeks.

The tears worked as collyrium
further cleansing your eyes
on one hand,
and on the other hand
wrapping my eyes
with colossal gloom
everlastingly.

Unburden yourself

Let those in paradise suffer,
who in the desire of bliss
and beatitude
led an unsullied life on Earth.

Let those in hell enjoy,
who didn't give a damn
about the other world
and who had the nerve
to pilot their lives
the way they seemed fit.

A man
who is indifferent
to both paradise and hell
and to all moral dualities -
such a man can only do good,
the good being the right thing,
the right being the only choice possible
for a justified action.

Go red

Every colour
at first
looks unique,
distinct,
and possessing a texture
of its own.

However,
on a second glance
it is found
that every colour
is a concoction
of other colours,
that its uniqueness
and distinctiveness
is relative,
that its texture
is a whole
made up
from the disintegration
and incorporation
of one
or more than one
of its constituent part.

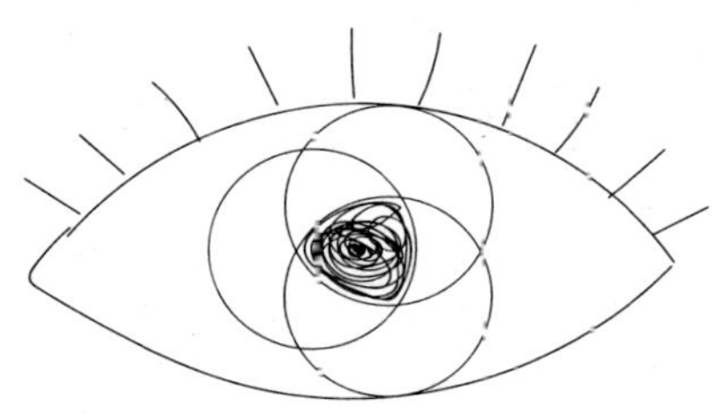

Acceptance

No shoulder
is worth weeping on,
so slurp up your tears,
roll up your sleeves
and strive to respire
without any restraint.

You came unaccompanied
and you'll go single-handedly
with an incredible amount of misery,
without knowing unerringly
why it all happened
in the first place.

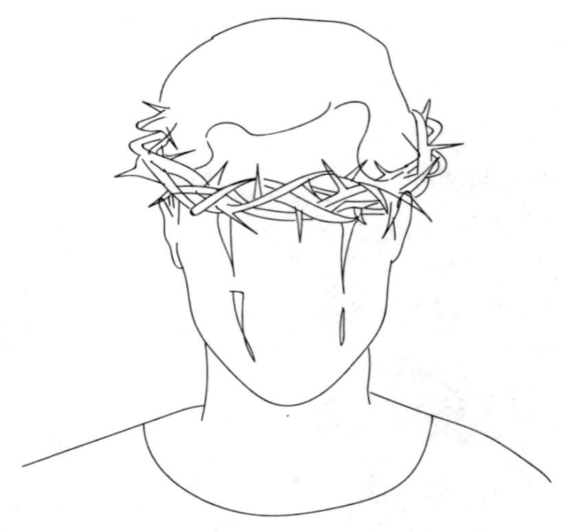

Shame on you dawn!

Oh dawn,
the sight of you
is so dismal
that even dusk
becomes susceptible
to vulnerability
at the slightest
thought of you.

You transport obscurity
in the lives of people
by generously giving them
a phoney hope of luminosity.

You seize all the glory
of the morning sunshine
but you are highly impenitent
of the unprecedented horrors
that night unleashes
on the creatures of this Earth.

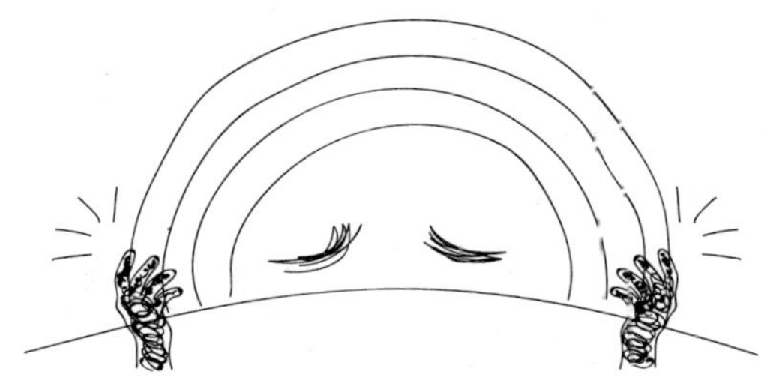

You (you) & I (i)

You say you are mine
and I say I am yours,
yet you are not mine
and I am not yours.

That which 'you' call YOU
is everything except YOU
and that which 'i' call I
is everything except I.

'Our' distorted
perception of
YOU and I
can only promise 'us'
a pseudo-image of US.

The authentic YOU
is all-inclusive of I
and the authentic I
is all-inclusive of YOU.

Hence,
in being YOU,
'you' will become I
and in being I,
'i' will become YOU.

Wishful nostalgia

Today I am missing
myself a lot,
being absent
physically,
mentally,
and emotionally
from my own existence.

The nonexistent nature
of my being
has been
the only witness
of my existence
and the witnesser
has now died
inside me.

Conceivably,
in my childhood
I was very close to myself,
so close that
whatever I thought I was, I was
and whatever I thought I wasn't, I wasn't
but in the present
that which I am not, I am
and that which I was
is only a pale remembrance.

By calling it a dim reminiscence,
I am identifying myself
today.

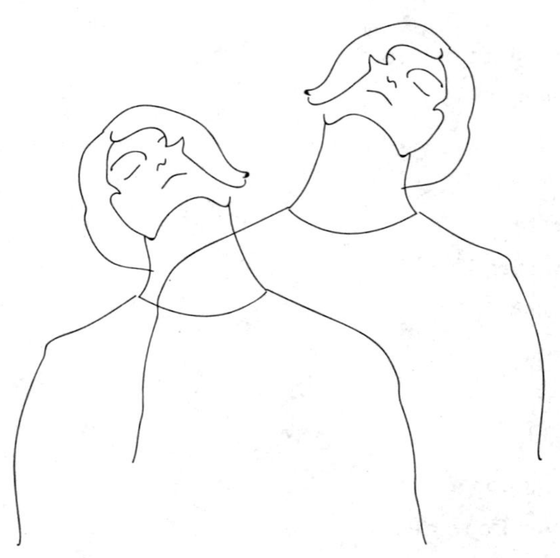

Was it hard for you?

What does it take
to simply 'love' individuals
for their virtue?

Don't you know
that material chattels
are like soap suds
which will peter out
in emaciated air
before you would recognize.

Don't you know
that death will seize
the material part of your existence,
the carcass.

A dazzling ornament
on a corpse is no good.

Thus,
become conscious
and be one
with that eternal gem,
the glow of which
radiates from every pore and cell
of your body;

that eternal 'Atman'[1]
which does not corrode
with the lapse of time.

1 Atman - the spiritual life principle of the universe, especially when regarded as immanent in the individual's real self.

An inimitable relationship

I and the ceiling fan
gaze at each other
all night long
without uttering a word.

Although,
I can put the fan in motion
with just a click of a button
but I fear
that like all human relations,
putting the fan in motion
for my own interest
will slacken its tie
with the ceiling (its roots)
and will make it collapse on me
with all its power -
leading to my death
or crippling me
and making me endure
like in love
till the end of my days.

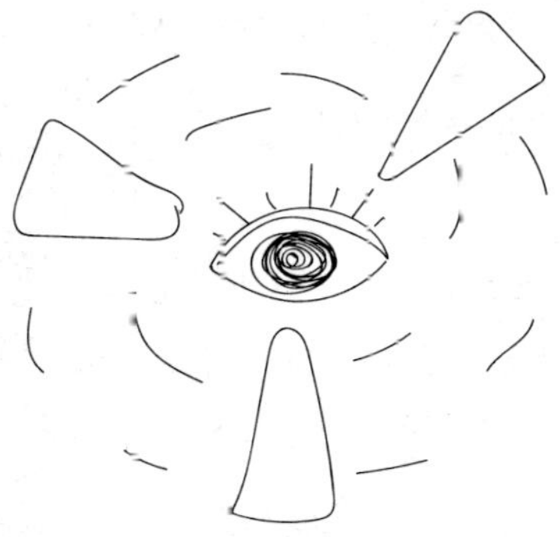

The purpose of writing

All writers
put pen to paper
in order to be able
to write that
which cannot be written.

An emotion
which no word
can put across
in any lingo.

Something
that is so close to them
and yet so far-flung
that no matter
how firmly they try,
it still remains stand-offish
but because of which
they become capable
of writing what they write.

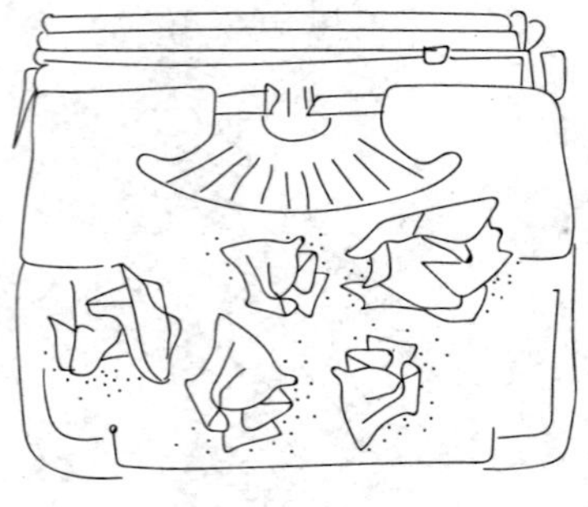

We are our own shadows

Initially,
while looking
at my own silhouette,
I discovered
that I exist.

But
I also discovered
that I exist
only as a form,
a manifestation
of some sort -
the loci
or the reference point
of this manifestation
being outside
and not inside of me,
that which I call ‘me’.

It is the outer
that creates
the inner
and not vice-versa.

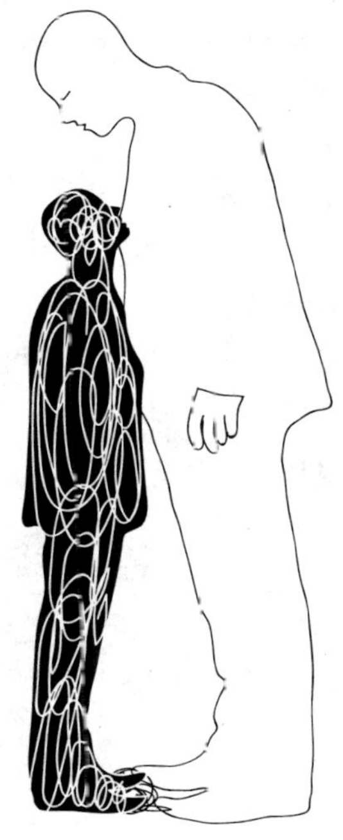

A love affair

Books are not
our best friends
but
our worst enemies.

They put ideas
in our mind,
ideas which are
not our own,
ideas which are alien,
ideas which besmirch
and bestow upon us
a false sense of being,
of identity,
of knowledge,
of truth,
of growth,
and of life.

Still, there is
a peculiar fondness
for books,
perhaps because
enemies are real
and friends are fake.

Stop complaining!

Can you look up
at the sky
without complaining?

To whom
do you complain
when you can't affirm anything
with certainty
about your own existence?

Do not reiterate
what Descartes said:
"I think
therefore I am".

Stumble upon it yourself
and pose the question 'how'
only if you have a desire
to be misled.

If you have found
a purpose in life,
well, keep it to yourself
and live with dignity.

However,
if you have failed
to find a purpose in life,
do whatever suits you -
smirk,
sob,
or be indifferent
but do not complain.

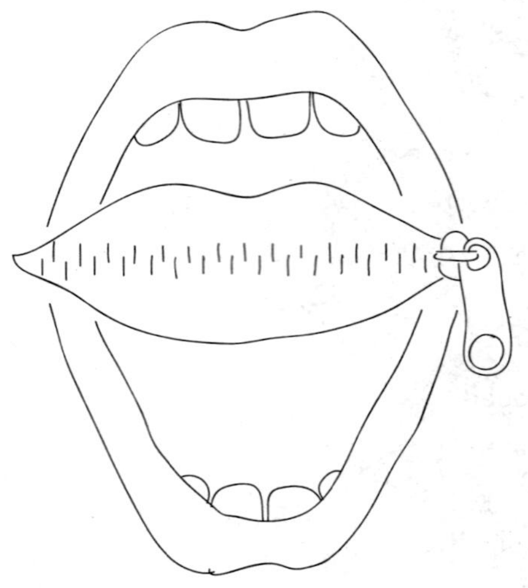

The dream is bigger than the dreamer

All organs in the human body
perform specific functions
but these functions
are more or less
for the survival
of the living organism.

Till the organism lives,
there is a potential
to transcend
the very state
it lives in.

An eye fulfils its purpose
when it sees
that which cannot be seen.

A nose fulfils its purpose
when it smells
that which cannot be smelled.

An ear fulfils its purpose
when it hears
that which cannot be heard.

A tongue fulfils its purpose
when it tastes
that which cannot be tasted.

The skin fulfils its purpose
when it touches
that which cannot be touched.

What is that
which cannot be
seen, smelled, heard,
tasted and touched?

Perhaps,
it is our true essential nature -
that which can only be experienced
when one,
who is wanting to experience it,
dies a physical death
and becomes one
with the experience.

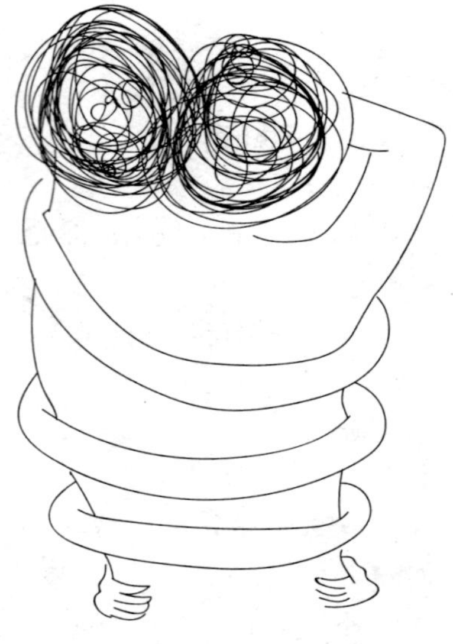

Voluntary exit

It was a black night
and all of a sudden
pain usurped
deep in my heart.

I desired
a glimmer of moonlight,
but my eyes bled instead.

I looked for some liquor
but every bottle
was found to be overflowing
with tears.

I drank the tears
and tried to suck the air
in a jiffy.

The cold took the indictment
of stirring the pain,
my hands and feet
became numb,
my heart was befuddled
as the cord of light
was kaput fully
and there was blackness
all around.

Assuming
that there is no one
in heaven
to eavesdrop my prayer,
I called out her name
for the very last time
and then took a deliberate egress
from this entrapment called life.

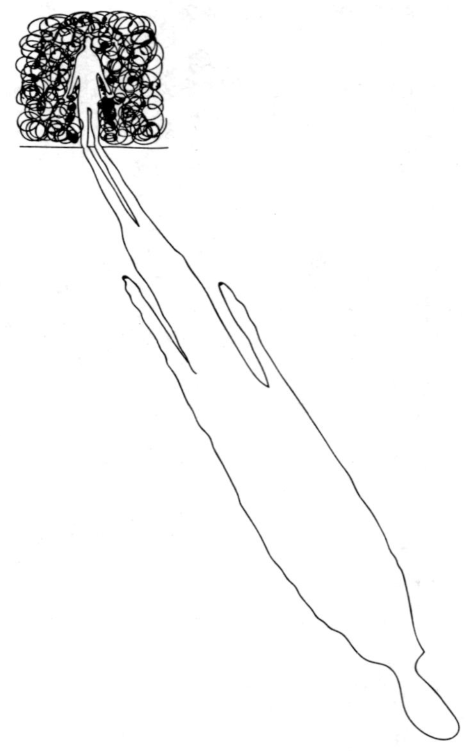

Slay

Kill me right away
if you wish
to make me immortal.

Even a slight delay
on your part
can cost me
another day of mortality.

So think about it
and do the needful.

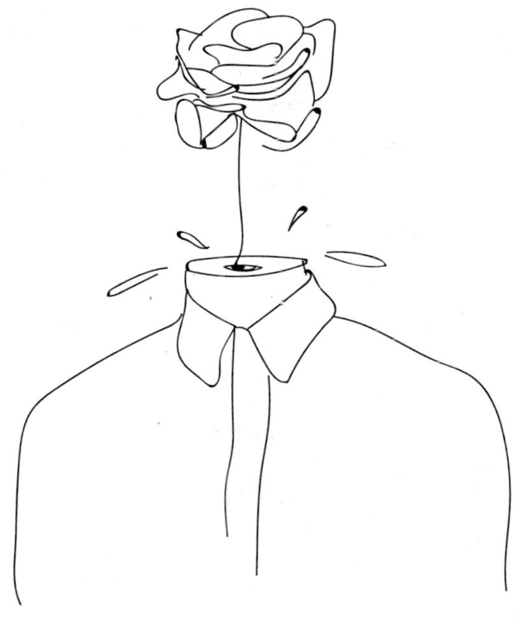

Camouflage

No season is deemed fit
to my temperament.

When I asked the clouds
for an unruffled cool breeze of air,
the sun in return
scalded my hair.

When I wished
for some sunshine
during the murky winter days,
arctic shivers went down
my spinal cord in twine.

When I desired for drizzle
and some lightening
in the sky,
the yellow foliage fell
from the trees nearby.

At last,
after giving up
all my hope,
I hopelessly romanticized
about my own death.

Unfortunately,
even that was counterfeited
instantaneously
in the form of life,
because of which
I am still alive
or have a chimaera
of being alive;
constantly blazing
and suffering
like a character in disguise.

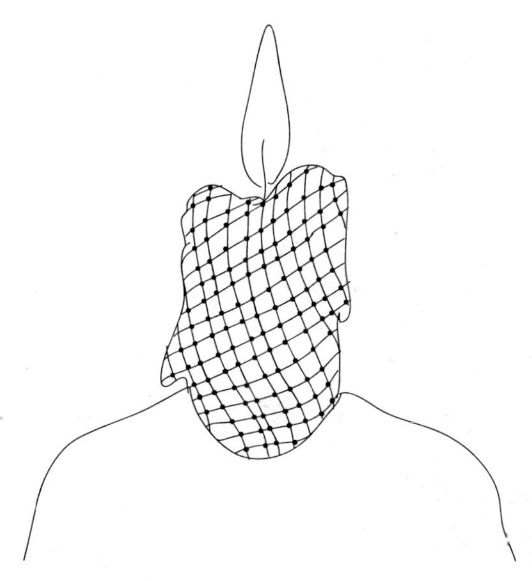

Freedom is bondage

We humans
desire freedom
more than anything;
more than love,
even more than virtue.

But has anyone
thought of freedom
as another kind of bondage?

The very concept of freedom
is borne
out of our incarcerated mind.

Hence,
our vision of freedom
is also constrained
by a certain frontier of thought
which defies the significance
of the very word
freedom stands for.

Also,
choice is a manipulated instrument;
we do not choose at will.

The underpinning
of the construction
of our will
is largely based
on what we are not
rather than
on what we are.

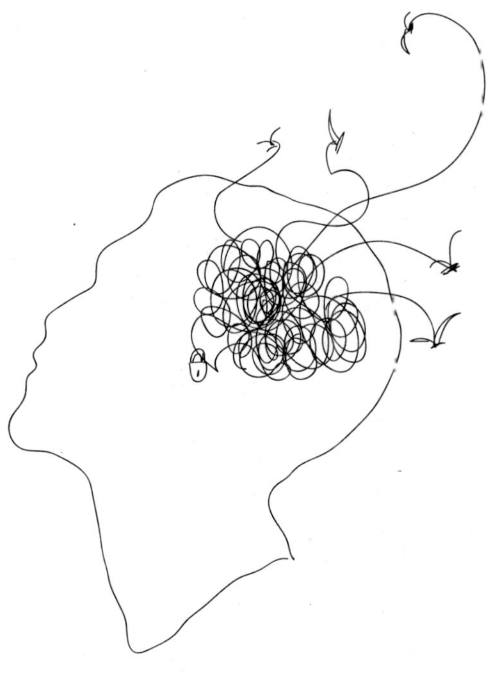

Lexis

Words are dumb
and the reader
is deaf.

The meaning
is akin to
cotton wrapped
in its own cover.

Just as cotton
burns away
at the hands of fire,
the meaning too
burns away
at the sight
of a reader.

Hence,
no communion
is likely possible
between the two
ever.

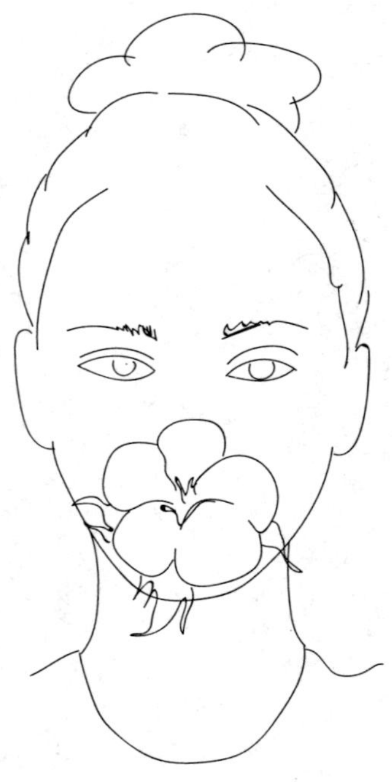

Desire

We desire
neither heaven
nor hell,
nor that
which lies
between heaven
and hell.

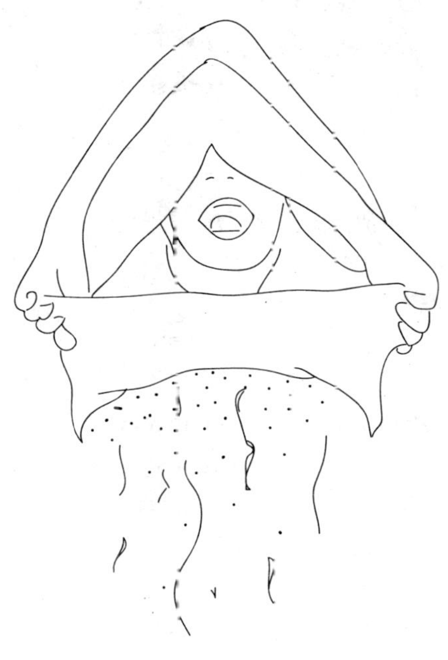

We desire
neither the sky
nor the Earth,
neither a beloved
nor a God,
neither any medicine
nor any prayers,
neither loyalty
nor hardship,
neither a fellow traveller
nor a guide,
and neither temporary pleasure
nor permanent pain.

All that we,
humble low born, desire
is a proper farewell
and an exit
from this entrapment
called life.

When in love

Only when you are in love,
you can shield yourself
from all the adversities
of life.

Only when you are in love,
you have the vigour
to surmount
all the devils inside you.

Only when you are in love,
you get an opportunity
to be a better version
of yourself.

Only when you are in love,
you have the audacity
to pronounce the truth
amid all the mendacity
that surrounds you.

Only when you are in love,
you are able to create something,
even out of the shattered
pieces of your existence.

Only when you are in love,
you for the very first time
feel alive
and even death
cannot kill you.

Only when you are in love,
'you' are actually not
and when 'you' are actually not,
'you' actually are.

Killing time is an art

Those who can't kill time,
can't do anything.

Killing time requires
all kinds of skills
one has acquired
over a period of a lifetime.

Killing time is not a joke,
it is a serious affair.

Those who know
how to kill time,
they know everything.

One has to be free of charge,
absolutely lighthearted
in order to kill time.

Our own thoughts
can become fatal
with little negligence.

Learn to kill time
before time kills you.

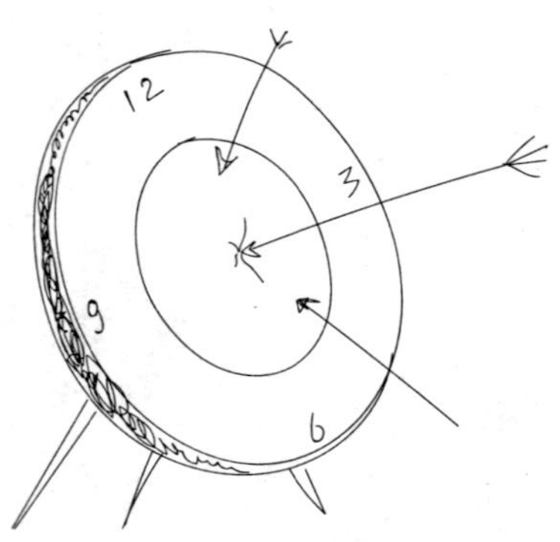

Face value

Never take anything
on its face value.

Face value are values
posited on things
to chip away
or to buttress
their true worth.

In each case,
the true reality
of the thing in itself
is intentionally
or unintentionally veiled.

Men and women themselves
are neither good nor bad
but there is a face value
they set on their character
which changes with time
depending upon the situation.

In short,
face values are prices
rather than values
which help people
in their day to day bargain.

It takes less than a moment

It takes
less than a moment
for an 'is'
to become a 'was'.

Everything that 'is'
in this moment
becomes
everything that 'was'
in the very next moment.

This 'isness' is life
and this 'wasness'
is the absence of life.

But
we can only talk
about this 'wasness'
through the prism of 'isness'.

Right now,
this poem 'is' being written
and once it is complete
it will be read as -
'was' written.

We are all born
into this 'isness'
and we all die
into this 'isness';
only memories linger
of the individual 'isness'
in terms of a collective 'wasness'.

Vice

The wicked
know the secret
which the good
is still searching for.

The wrong
will eventually
do the right thing
and the right
will eventually
do the wrong thing.

The ugly
was always beautiful
and the beautiful
was always ugly.

Weapons were invented
by the kind-hearted
while the cruel-hearted
died with trampled flowers
in their hands.

Those who think
this is not the way
how things are,
well, this is precisely the way
how things work.

Not because I assert it,
not because you refute it,
not because somebody
neither asserts or refutes it,
but because of the way
it is.

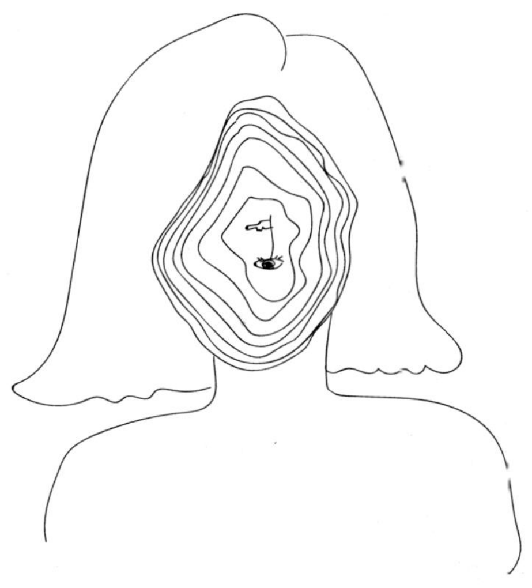

Life is not a hula hoop!

I went out
to feed the hungry
and came back
starving myself.

I went out
to feed the thirsty
and came back
parched myself.

I went out
to stitch someone's wound
and came back
with a sore myself.

I went out
to donate some clothes
and came back
naked myself.

I went out
to explore the garden of Eden
and came back
feeling dejected.

In life,
what goes around
never comes around.

The thoroughfare of life
is one-directional;
what goes,
goes forever
and what stays,
stays forever.

Dirge

The only thing
worth mastering
in this life
on this Earth
is the art of crying.

There is nothing
more soothing
in this world
than howling your heart out.

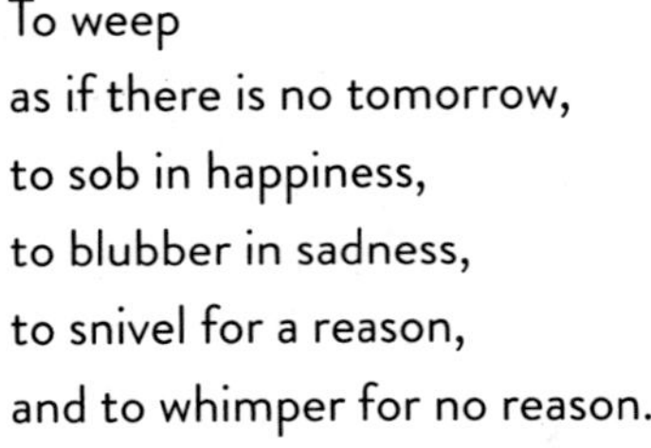

To weep
as if there is no tomorrow,
to sob in happiness,
to blubber in sadness,
to snivel for a reason,
and to whimper for no reason.

To shed tears in one's own pain,
to bawl in someone else's pain,
and to wet one's garment
with tears of blood.

To be born while lamenting,
to live while weeping,
and to die while howling.

Enlightenment

Look at the sky
and look at the Earth.

Look at the sun
and look at the moon.

Look at the clouds
and look at the stars.

Look at the thunder
and look at the lightening.

Look at the rain
and look at the rainbow.

Look at the day
and look at night.

Look at the trees
and look at the flowers.

Look at the birds
and look at the animals.

Look at the famine
and look at the drought.

Look at your father
and look at your mother.

Look at your brother
and look at your sister.

Look at your friend
and look at your lover.

Look at your children
and look at your grandchildren.

Look at your body
and look at your soul.

Look! Till there is
nothing left to look.

Look! Till you are
no longer able to look.

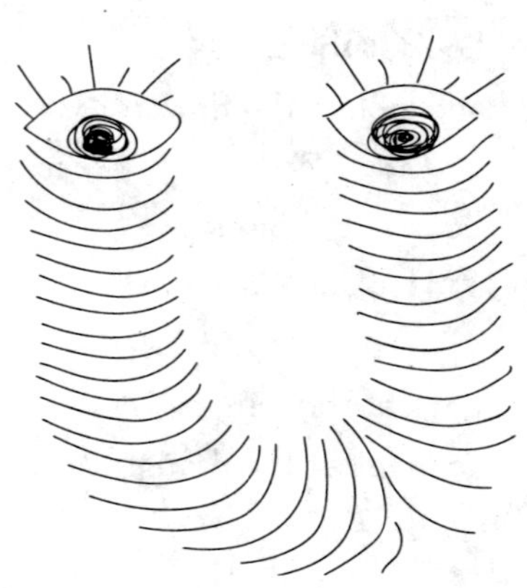

Farewell

Unfortunately,
my liver has aged
and has become fatty
due to excessive drinking;
a punishment,
which in the name of joy
many men like me
inflict on themselves.

My lungs have aged
and have become corroded
due to excessive smoking;
a punishment,
which in the name of joy
many men like me
inflict on themselves.

My kidneys have aged
and have shrunken
due to binge eating;
a punishment,
which in the name of joy
many men like me
inflict on themselves.

But fortunately,
my heart has remained
as young as a newborn child's
due to its undying ability
to wonder,
to feel more than others -
all kinds of emotions
in all situations of life.

Come,
meet me people
and bid me goodbye
from whatever remains
of your young hearts.

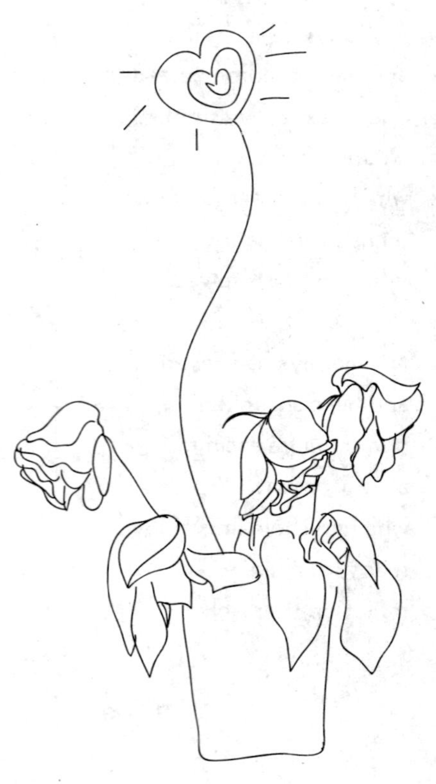

It

Hear it
in whichever way
you can hear it.

See it
in whichever way
you can see it.

Smell it
in whichever way
you can smell it.

Touch it
in whichever way
you can touch it.

Taste it
in whichever way
you can taste it.

Feel it
in whichever way
you can feel it.

Name it
in whichever way
you can name it.

Call it
in whichever way
you can call it.

But
do not ask me
what is 'it'
because that defeats
the whole rationale
behind it.

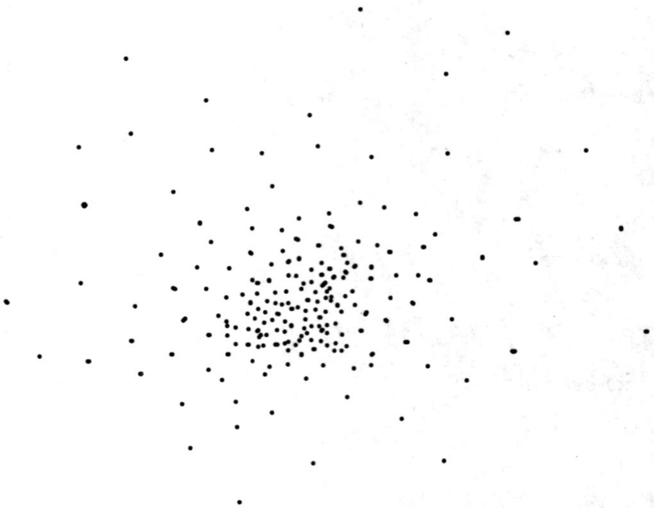

A photograph

A dazzling bright photograph
hanging droopily
on the wall of my room
at times takes me
on a voyage
in another
dreamlike world;
in a world wherein,
nothing is at my disposal
and where
only two or three barren trees
are visible.

Few women
can be seen
holding a bow and arrow
in their hands
and few men
can also be seen
lying down in pain,
feeling disconsolate.

The thought of these people
brings me back to myself
and I find myself crying
while sitting amid books
scattered all over the place
in a miserly gloomy room.

Maybe

As a child,
I always contemplated
what life is all about?

I never thought
that it was that intricate
a question.

Although
people in every generation
have tried to answer
in their own way
what life is all about,
this question
in itself is absurd.

In fact,
to ask this question
is to embark
on an expedition
of non-comprehension.

All questions
are essentially
the shadows
of the answers
we already have.

The answers
go on changing
with time
but the questions
remain the same.

If life
is all about being animate,
then we all are in a way
a symbol of life,
but are we alive?

What does it mean
to be alive?

Perhaps
we are unaware of it.

That
which is speaking
through me,
is that me?

If that is presumed
to be me,
then what would you call
the intermediate space
between that and me?

Is life
a name
given to signify
everlasting love?

Is life
a name
given to signify
the remembrance
of our distant past?

Is life
a name
given to signify
the weariness
and fatigue
caused by the outcome
of months and years
in succession?

Is life
a name
given to signify
a glorious future?

Maybe
this question is wrong.

Maybe
this life is wrong.

Maybe I am wrong.

Maybe you are wrong.

Inauthentic mode of living

Each day
ends with night
and each night we sleep
with tremendous faith
that we will wake up
the next morning
the same way
as we went to sleep
the last night -
awake and breathing.

We stake so much
on our sleep
and on our dreams;
an unconscious state of being
on which
we have no control.

Yet we discard
our encounter
with our cognizant state
and are frightened
to die at any moment.

Marriage

If I ever tie the knot
and if I ever have children,
I want them
to abhor me
for two reasons.

First,
because hate
is purer
than love.

Second,
because if my children
happen to love me,
then they will never be able
to live their own lives
as they will always mourn
thinking about
all that their father
had been through
in his life,
long after I perish
from Earth.

Parents strive
to shield their children
from all kinds of
dark veiled ugly truths
by always seeking a chance
to colour their inevitable pessimism
through refined optimism.

I don't wish to colour
anything for my children.

If I have any ever
and if they hate me,
well and good;
it will be in the best interest
for all of us
as father and children.

Ego is a bitch!

In my childhood,
there were many teachers
who used to beat the students
when they smiled and laughed;
I was one of them.

When I used to get thrashed
on the pretext of laughing,
I used to think
that what kind of educators are they
who beat children for smiling.

Those teachers though
had matured in age
but they still couldn't detach
their thoughts from their ego.

Their own insecurities
made them believe
that in all cases it was them
who were being made fun of
by the students.

In the garb of knowledge,
they thought they had every right
to treat the young souls
the way they wanted
and deemed it
as a favour unto them.

But any person,
especially a teacher
who thrashes someone
for smiling and laughing
is a curse
on this benevolent Earth.

A smile and some laughter
is all that there is
to the vitality of human life.

Any restriction on it,
irrespective of the situation
and circumstance,
should be condemned
with effect from now.

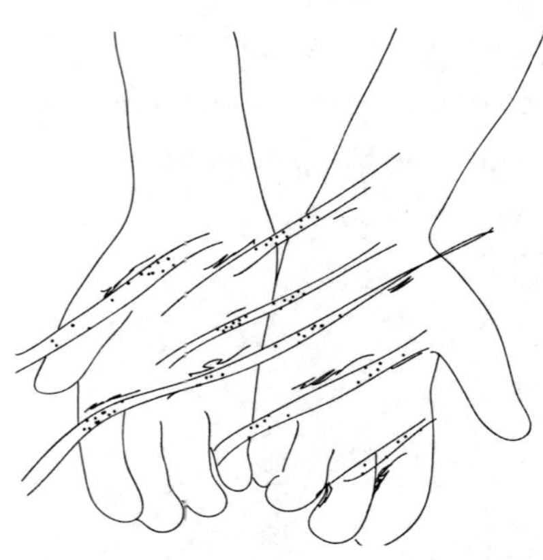

Think twice

In the evening,
don't step outside the house.

The evening approaches
to appease no one;
neither the morning
nor the day,
neither the night
and not even itself.

Its only purpose
of arrival each day
is to hoodwink
the humankind into believing
that we are just bodies
which will perish
in ashes one day
as our time on Earth
is limited.

It murmurs in our ears swiftly
that our bodies have failed
time and again
to bear the weight
of our thoughts.

But the evening doesn't discern
that there is another world
where only our thoughts
can reach and exist,
where the body is not required
for the thoughts to exist,
where the thought is itself action,
where the evening, morning,
day and night are all fused
into one indivisible timelessness.

Till you exist as a body
on this Earth,
beware of the evening!

I object

My whole purpose
of writing anything
is to contradict –
the first statement
with the second,
the second statement
with the third,
so on and so forth,
till there is nothing left
to contradict further.

My whole purpose
of writing anything
is to make myself
totally perplexed
to a point where
I become clear
about the nature
of my thoughts.

My whole purpose
of writing anything
is to draw myself
nearer to the 'truth',
without knowing
what the 'truth' is
and the only way

I could do it
in my understanding
is by contradicting myself
like life itself,
to say yes than a no
or to say no than a yes;
being both right and wrong
at the same time
or being
neither right nor wrong -
to live beyond extremes
in-between words.

Hurt

Of all the people I have met
and of all the relationships
that I have been into,
everyone has ended up
hurting me
in one way or the other
and I have ended up
hurting everyone
in one way or the other
as I am told.

Hurt is the only outcome
of every thought/action,
whether passive or active.

Being scared of getting hurt
is like
being afraid of something
you have no control on
whatsoever
and there is nothing
you can do about fear.

The same fear
that shields you
kills you
by the process of inaction.

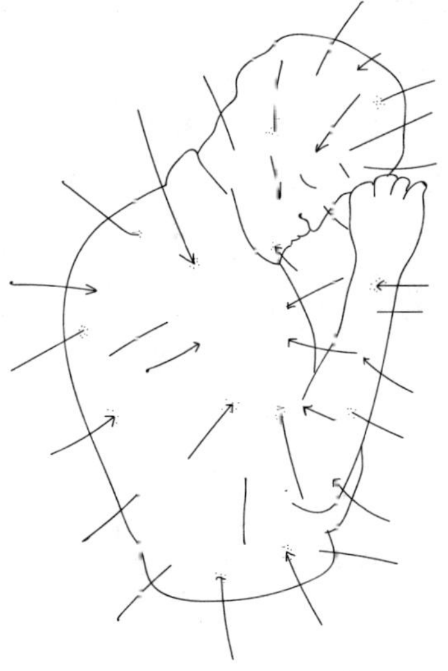

Nobody tells

The rays of the sun
often cast
a non-penetrable
darkness in me.

It is often said
that the veil of darkness
can be lifted
through light
but if the light
starts to radiate darkness,
what is
to be done?

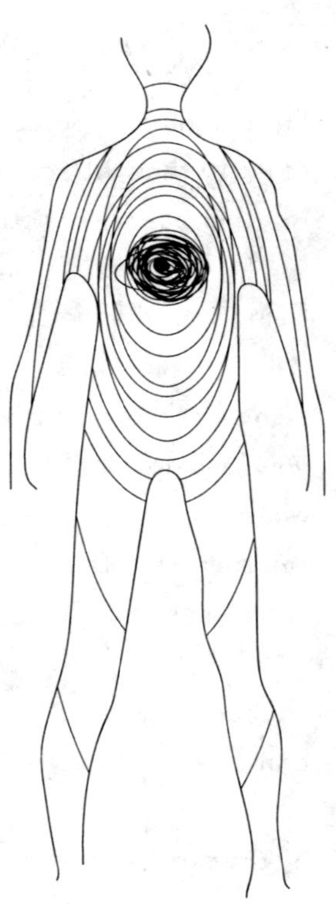

Monochrome

The spectacle,
the view,
or the scene
spread all across nature
can either be
completely black
or
completely white
or
of a shade
non-recognizable
between pure black
and pure white.

All other colours emerge
as figments of imagination,
an illusion of some sort.

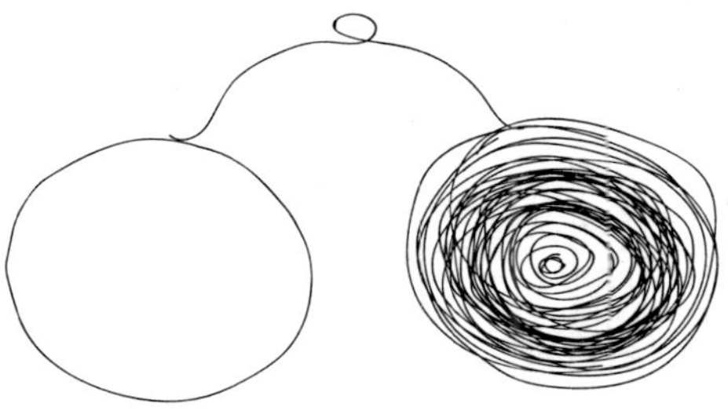

My eyes have seen everything

There is nothing
that my eyes haven't seen.

My eyes have seen
a newborn baby
in the lap of the mother,
feeling as secure and contented
as a tender sapling feels
in the lap of mother Earth.

My eyes have seen
adolescent boys and girls
spending all their time
in discovering new ways
to release their sexual tension.

My eyes have seen
adults complaining about
the loss of youth and innocence
and cribbing about
middle age crisis.

My eyes have seen
aged people in illness,
suffering on their death bed,
feebly wailing for help
from everyone they see.

My eyes have seen
poverty, hunger,
murders, rapes,
and abuses of all kinds.

My eyes have also seen
a few great masters
who whitewashed death
while being alive.

But one thing
that my eyes
are yet to encounter
is my own death,
which I cannot escape
like the few great masters.

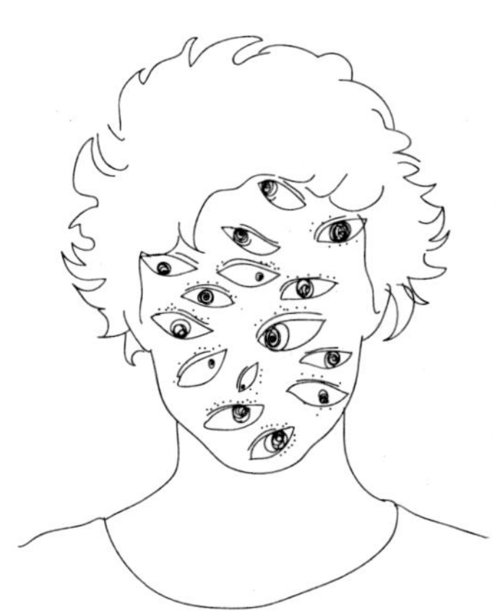

The black diary

After I die,
you must open my almirah
and look for the black diary
in which I wrote many poems.

I want you to take those poems
to a well-known publisher
and get them published.

I assure you
that you will not face any trouble
in reading all that I wrote
as my handwriting has always been fair.

Also, you don't even have to hire an editor
as I have already edited everything
and compiled it all in this diary.

As to the question
why I want you to publish these poems?

Well,
whatever that might get published in my name
with your strenuous effort,
it wouldn't be of any aid to me;
neither in monetary terms
nor in terms of notoriety and reverence
as I would already be dead by then.

But if whatever good I wrote gets published,
then it may enlighten some other individuals like me
and might save them from committing suicide.

I found my first and last refuge in poetry
whenever I was sunk in the thought of suicide.

Maybe my written words save someone somewhere;
to get saved completely is to die fully.

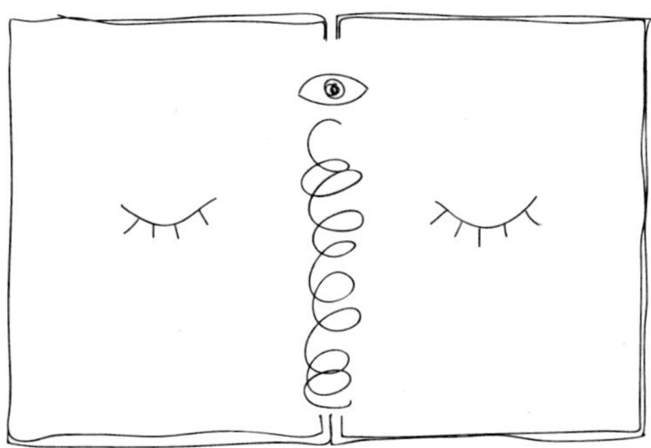

Rest in peace

Since the day
my father passed away,
all the flowers and plants
in the house,
which he had kept so graciously,
started to die gradually.

I, on my own part
did everything
to keep them alive.

I watered them adequately,
kept them in tolerable sunlight
and shade
and did all that was essential
but still,
they withered away before time.

Perhaps, probably, for sure,
I think that
what I couldn't provide them
was my 'love'.

One can only give that
what one has.

I was too empty inside
to feel anything,
any sort of emotion
at that point in time.

I was too empty inside
to give anything,
any sort of comfort
that would qualify
as true love.

Everything minus love
becomes nothing
in no time
and nothing plus love
becomes everything
gradually.

My father

My father
would have been proud
to see and know
that now I wake up
early in the morning,
no matter how late I sleep
at night.

My father
would have been proud
to see and know
that I finally took a job,
something which I always considered
highly unsettling and upsetting,
especially in the kind of world
we live in now.

My father
would have been proud
to see and know
that now I sensibly attend to my duties
towards my mother and sister,
no matter how irresponsible
I have been
all throughout my life.

My father
would have been proud
to see and know
that my first book of poetry
is about to get published soon.

My father
would have been proud
to see and know
that I am not dead yet
and via me
he lives too,
giving continuity
to my life.

Meaninglessness

There is nothing
to utter today
in thoughts,
in words,
and in feelings.

Still, I am writing,
what should be done in such a case?

Maybe I should just unite the words
and leave the space between two words blank -
where the meaning is often found.

Then I should wish
that probably,
as life itself emerges in water,
in the same way,
the meaning might emerge
on its own
out of the spaces
that I have left blank knowingly
between the two words.

Maybe
I should just leave it
to the readers,
to plug in their own meaning
in those empty spaces
between the two words
with the fullness of matter
within their bodily nomenclature.

Or maybe
I should just
leave it meaningless,
as all things are left
in the end.

Parched

It took me
almost a lifetime
to realize
that the things
I have been using
or in fact, abusing
in order to fight depression,
in order to fix anxiety disorders,
in order to quench my eternal thirst
propelled by life itself,
in order to breathe and survive
like normal human beings;
all of this has over the years
only made me
more depressed,
more anxious,
more thirsty,
and more incapable
to breathe and survive
like normal human beings.

It feels like
I was better off before.

Now
I have reached
a point of no return
and I am more thirsty
than ever before.

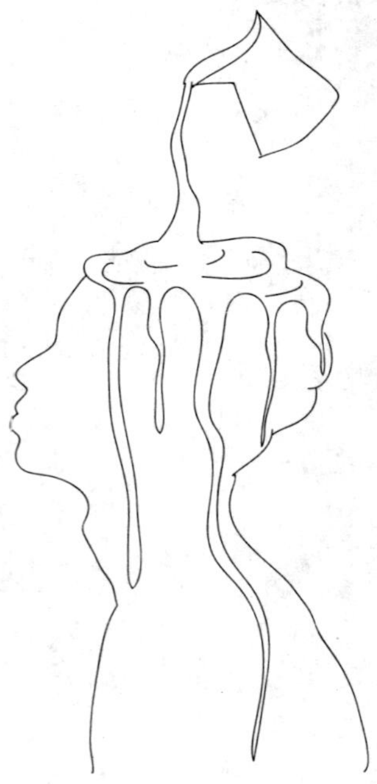

Gallows

There is something
worth noticing
about the palms
of beautiful girls.

There is something
that is concealed in them,
which only becomes apparent
after a deliberate careful
perception.

These palms
like a chessboard
are a complete map
of the battlefield.

To my poetic eyes,
these fixed marked lines
on the palms
appear to be a queue in which
mad lovers are standing from eternity
with their plea
but because they themselves
are a part of the queue,
they cannot separate themselves
from the queue
and look at their own selves
to pass any remark.

These palms are nothing
but gallows in which
the shrills of
uncountable number of suitors
have been silenced.

The palms have turned red
with the blood of the suitors
but the palms don't appear red
and in fact, appear
as bright as the afternoon sun -
maybe because
to see the darkness
beneath the candle,
it is imperative to stub out
the flame of the candle
but the flame enlightened
in the palms of beautiful girls
cannot be extinguished
as it is not lit up by wax
but by the blood of suitors.

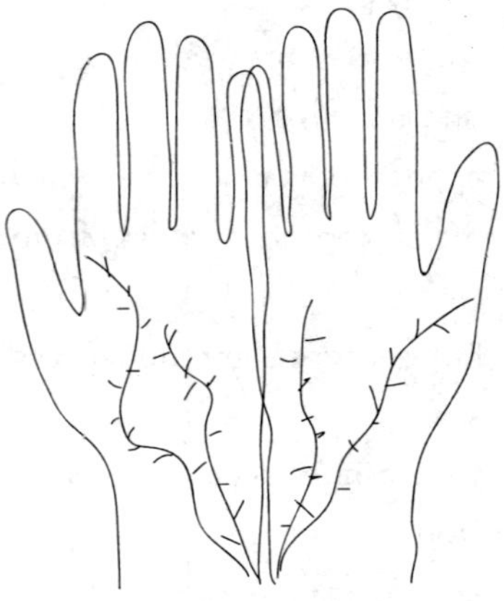

Muse

Inspiration
is like perspiration.

When individuals
surrender themselves
to the scorching sun,
they perspire.

The same way,
when individuals
surrender themselves
to non-dualistic thoughts,
they get inspired.

As the sweat of each individual
has its own distinct odour and taste,
the inspiration of each individual
has its own source of inspiration.

My inspiration
is the non-dualistic thought
of the scorching sun
which makes me perspire
all the time.

The vacuum of fear

As soon as I close my eyes,
unprecedented horrors abound me -
first in sounds
and then in visuals,
as if my whole body
has turned into a vacuum of fear.

I see people who I have lost
and I see people whom I have never met -
all of them pointing towards an abyss,
making me see the futility of life;
the struggle of inhaling and exhaling
without a cause.

Even in the dream state,
the witnesser inside me
knows it's a dream
and no matter how sturdily
the witnesser wants to drag me out of the dream,
the dream pulls me more and more inside of her,
suffocating me further,
till I open my eyes again.

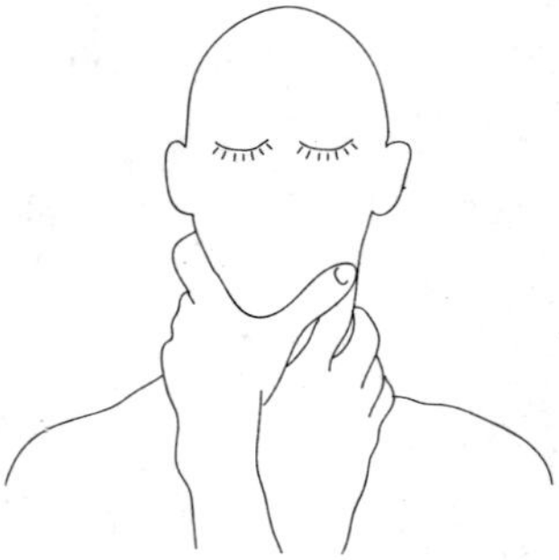

The art of writing

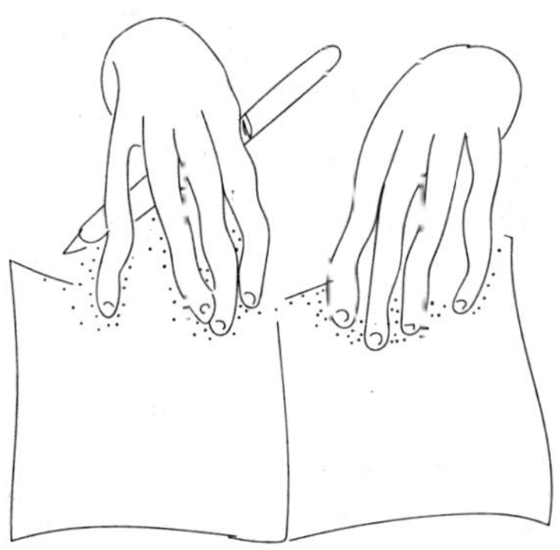

Do not write
just for the sake of writing.

Words too,
like human beings,
abhor each other
in the pretext of love.

When forced
and put together
out of sheer lack of passion,
they stink.

They stink
like burnt polythene;
the stench of which
the readers inhale
and the taste of their mouths
becomes appalling
when they read them.

The art of writing
is like gargling
with saline water
but the writer uses words
instead of saline water
and spits it out only
when the blisters of inconsistency
are cured by consistent thought.

Congregation

Living individuals
in their lives
must have asked the question -
where do dead people go?

The predicament is
that there is no answer
to this question;
neither was there an answer
in the past,
neither is there an answer
in the present
and nor is there going to be
an answer in the future.

In order to know
where dead people go,
one must die.

When I die,
only then I will know
where dead people go
and if I am fortunate enough,
I might even get to meet everyone
whom I lost in my life,
much prior
than I anticipate.

For all those
who might seek me out
after I am gone,
well, probably,
you all can meet me too
after your respective deaths
at the same place
where all people meet
after death.

If, then...

If I had to follow Christianity,
then I would prefer to be
a Protestant Christian.

If I had to follow Islam,
then I would prefer to be
a Shia Muslim.

If I had to follow Atheism,
then I would prefer to be
an Agnostic Atheist.

If I had to follow Hinduism,
then I would prefer to be
a Shaiva Hindu.

If I had to follow Buddhism,
then I would prefer to be
a Hinayana Buddhist.

If I had to follow Sikhism,
then I would prefer to be
a Nirankari Sikh.

If I had to follow Judaism,
then I would prefer to be
a Hiloni Jew.

If I had to follow Jainism,
then I would prefer to be
a Digambar Terapanth Jaina.

If I had to follow Zoroastrianism,
then I would prefer to be
a Restorationist Parsi.

But, I am glad
that I am not bound to follow
and I am not bound to choose.

The preliminary condition 'if'
doesn't apply to my state of existence
and without the 'if' condition,
the 'then' condition becomes redundant.

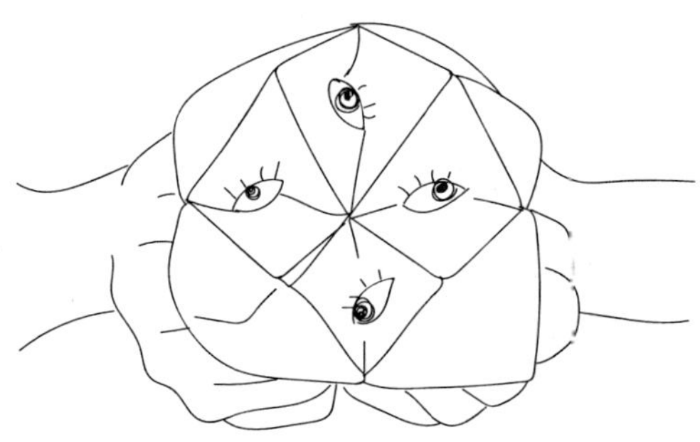

The muse of inspiration

A blank screen,
a blinking cursor,
one hand
on the keyboard,
one hand
holding a cigarette,
some music
in the background,
a cup of tea,
and a vulnerable evening -
an excuse
for not being able to write,
a writer's block perhaps!

Amidst all this,
the muse of inspiration
coming to the rescue,
taking all the blame
in the end.

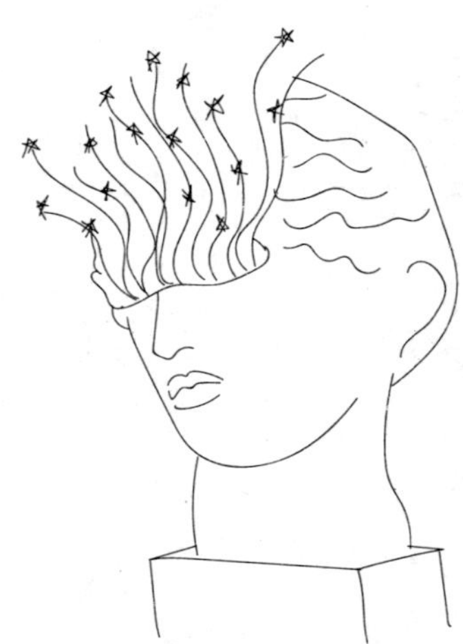

Be lost

Even though
all roads guide back home,
nobody ever arrives home.

We all go astray
somewhere in the way.

To be lost
is our essential nature.

One feels more perturbed
after reaching the destination
than one feels along the way
during the journey.

Those fortunate enough
who reach close to their real home,
they deny its very existence
due to their faint resemblance
and remembrance of it.

Migration does awful things
to people all around the world.

I can't even say
that never leave home.

Perhaps,
leaving home (comfort zone)
and suffering for a lifetime
is the best we can do.

Have faith in what I say

Don't augment my tribulations
by contradicting me
as already there are
innumerable troubles in life.

I am geared up to accept
everything you say
on the pretext
that you acknowledge
the only thing that I say -
to live with love
and not craft a concern
all the time.

This life,
this breath,
won't be there for long.

Make use of this breath
while you still can.

The secret of this cosmos
lies in the breath;
while you inhale and exhale,
witness your breath.

In solitude, sometimes,
there will be ample time
to pester and fight
when we continue to exist
as consciousness perhaps!

But till we have a body
to manifest our spirit -
just love, love and love
and have faith
in what I say.

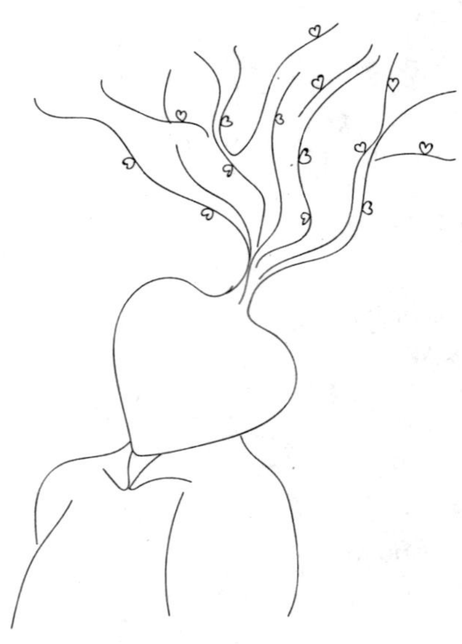

We die into this

Everything is served in courtrooms
except for justice.

Everything is served in schools and colleges
except for education.

Everything is served in marriages
except for love.

Everything is served in hospitals
except for cure.

Everything is served in hotels and restaurants
except for privacy.

Everything is served in zoos
except freedom.

Everything is served in old age homes
except for care.

Everything is served in prisons
except for punishment.

Everything is served in democracies,
except liberty.

Everything is served in churches, mosques,
temples, monasteries, synagogue and gurudwaras
except for the truth.

Everything is served in life
except for life.

Everything is served in death
except death.

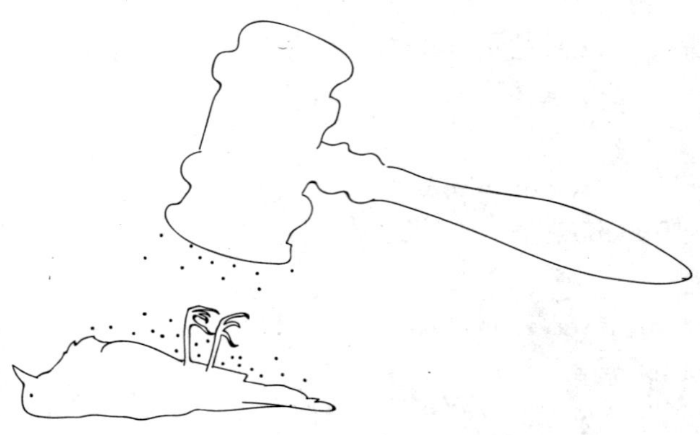

The difference

The poetry speaks itself about the poet
and each word states clearly
with what purpose and intent
it has been written by the so-called 'poet'.

I don't like poets
who cackle and grin all the time
as there is no cloaked wisdom in that,
irrespective of what their dreary optimism dictates them.

I don't like poets
who are egocentric;
the ones who write to advertise and sell,
the ones who write to fill their coffers with money,
and the ones who write for notoriety and respect.

I don't like poets
who read in large gatherings;
the ones who make a spectacle of their poetry,
the ones who always only read out their representative poems,
and the ones who recite less and spit more
to generate a wider response among the audience.

I don't like poets
who don't drink and smoke;
the ones who are afraid to die,
the ones who want to live a long successful life,
and the ones who themselves call themselves 'poets'.

I like poets
who cry all the time,
who howl their heart out
wherever they go,
who embrace the glumness of life,
and who denounce phoney sanguinity.

I like poets
who are altruistic in their nature,
who write for themselves,
and who write for the contentment
of their own heart, mind and soul.

I like poets
who don't read their own verse
but are always appreciative
of the poetry of other individuals
and if the need be -
those who read only in small gatherings,
who read out diverse chunks of poetry,
who recite more than the audience can chew,
and who feel pleased
if no one understands and reacts to their poetry.

I like poets
who indulge in all sorts of madness;
whether it is the use of some substance
or other means to nourish their creativity,
who don't wish for a long joyful life,

who themselves never call themselves 'poets',
who are not terrified of death,
who consider death as their darling,
and who wait for their union with death
till they breathe their last.

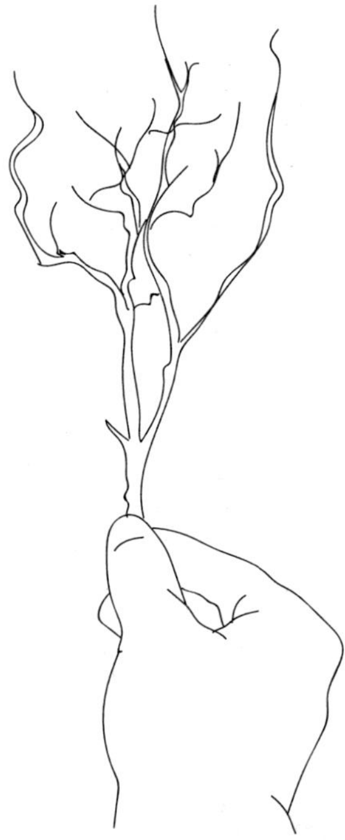

1+1 = 1

I occasionally speculate
as to what remained with me
and what all did I lose
in this life?

After thinking tersely,
I always arrive at an open conclusion
that whatever I gained in this life
is forever lost
and whatever I lost in this life
is what has lingered with me
till now.

I lost my infancy
at the hands of youth
and lost my youth
at the hands of adulthood
but both my childhood
and adulthood have
remained with me till now -
keeping me grounded on this Earth;
helping me measure the timeline of my life
on the timeline of eternity.

I lost my father unexpectedly,
a rare nerve disease killed him
and I thought I wouldn't live anymore
but life gave me strength
in the most brittle moments.

Me,
being the youngest,
the most sensitive
and emotional in the family,
had to become the eldest,
and the most dependable in those moments.

It was all made possible
by the sheer vigour of what remained
of my father with me
in the form of memories.

I also lost three of my girlfriends
to shitheads;
one of whom I actually loved
with all my heart and soul
but it is a thing of the past now.

I wish
that all the bad memories
that have haunted me
for several years
shall finally be reinstated
with good memories
by my fourth girlfriend,
who I hope will be
my last tangible love.

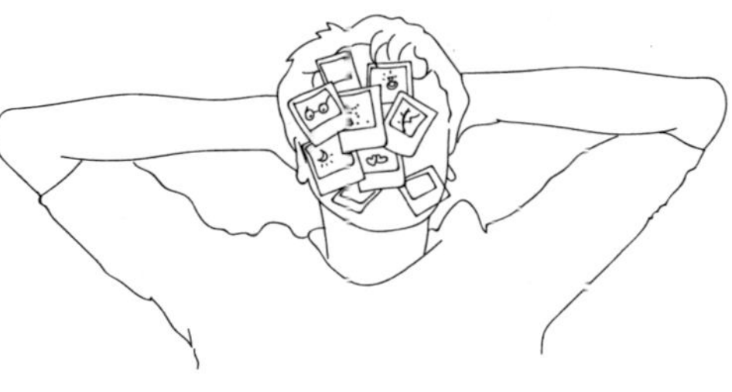

Virtue

If I ever have to commit a crime,
I would want to commit a crime
that would qualify my crime
as the most heinous act of this century
and that would label me
as the most 'atrocious' individual
of this century.

Any crime
which doesn't qualify for the death penalty
is a dim-witted act of ignorance and shame.

I know
what you all might be thinking
but I am not guilty
for I have not committed a crime.

So shut up!
I said shut up!
Stop judging!

Give me a fresh page now
as I wish to write a new poem.

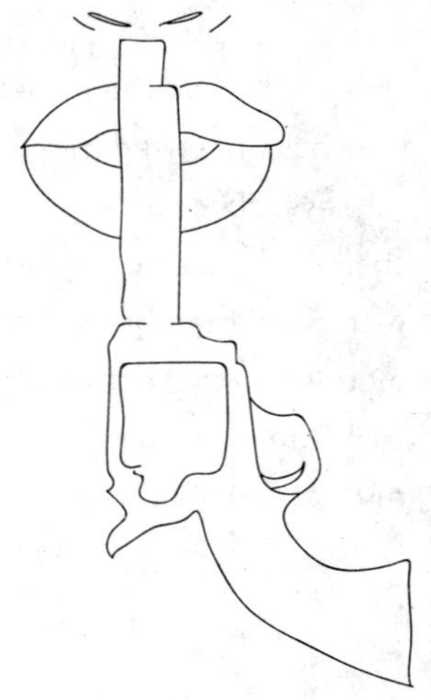

Regret

I reside
in the heart and mind
of each individual
and I travel on each breath.

I am born
when an individual is born
and I die
when an individual dies.

I am not a thought
as all thoughts are variations
that emerge
from my active passivity.

Some people call me
with another name - 'life'.

You heard that right,
sounds familiar?

But life is a false thought
arisen out of me
to make your lives habitable.

No matter what your names are,
you all are my progeny.

I am your only father
and your only mother.

My name is REGRET.

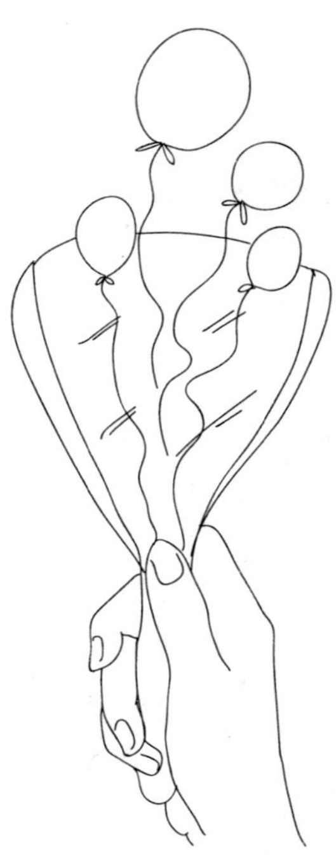

Now I know

Now I know
why all your boyfriends left you
and why all my girlfriends left me.

We humans
are not made for each other;
no two individuals in this world
are made for each other.

A man needs a woman
and a woman needs a man
like a butterfly needs a flower
and a flower needs a butterfly.

A butterfly sticks to the flower
to extort as much life-juice it can
from the flower
and the flower
feels as ecstatic as the butterfly
by allowing the butterfly
to suck it dry.

All the flowers belong
to all the butterflies in the world
and all the butterflies belong
to all the flowers in the world.

None of the butterflies belong
individually to a particular flower
and none of the flowers belong
individually to a particular butterfly.

We all belong to each other
collectively
like the butterfly and the flower
but none of us belong to each other
individually.

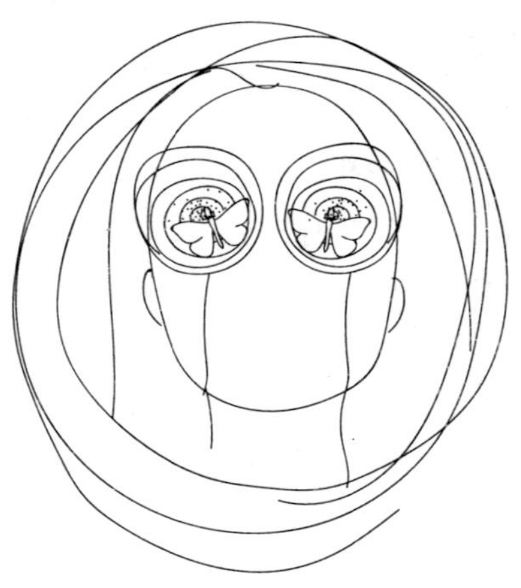

The drudgery of my life

These days,
after waking up in the morning,
I straightaway go to my office
without consuming anything.

These days,
I book an Uber
as my hands wobble
when I drive on my own.

After reaching the workplace,
I strive to work as much as possible
with whatever is assigned to me,
while at other times
I am lost in vain thoughts.

In the afternoon,
a cup of tea is served,
which I drink dispassionately
and even after possessing
a regular pack of cigarettes in my pocket,
I don't feel like going out
on a smoke break.

As hours pass by,
evening disembarks
with all its unsettled dues
and percolates inside me
for the next couple of hours,
before I finally book an Uber again
to a nearby tavern.

I buy
whatever I feel like drinking that day
and stand in the corner somewhere -
feeling crestfallen like always.

While I am sipping my pegs,
ignorant superfluous people
encircle me.

My eyes and ears
see and listen to things;
'things' which are absolute trash -
something on which
you can neither laugh nor cry.

Anyways,
after drinking and smoking
to my heart's content,
I finally return home
and without eating again,
I crawl to my bed.

Just before
I am about to fall asleep,
my mother comes to my room
and says: Son,
tomorrow don't leave home
before eating anything.

Laugh without a reason

In this world,
most people giggle
and weep
without any reason.

To laugh
and cry with reason
makes us realize
of our responsibilities
as conscientious citizens.

Then,
the reason
for mirth and sadness
doesn't exist anymore;
both the words
start to seem irrelevant
and tantamount
to one another.

That is why,
maybe,
there is a point
why people laugh and cry
without a reason.

I will also try
to laugh
without a reason,
as I have already cried a lot
without a reason.

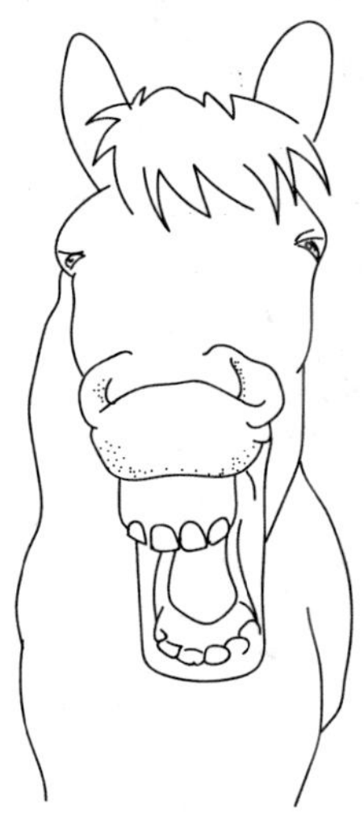

The power of thoughts

The habit of reading
a particular line
again and again,
whether of prose or poetry,
makes us realize what power
a thought can have on us
when expressed
through the right words.

For example,
I may say
that the day and moment
any two individuals
form a relation,
that particular day and moment
their relationship ends;
although the two individuals
involved in the relationship
realize it later.

In the same way,
I may say
that nobody dies of the cause
they fear the most.

I am sure,
you as readers
might agree or disagree
with the above two statements
but you cannot ignore them.

It will make you think,
even for a minute,
and you might feel compelled
to read them again.

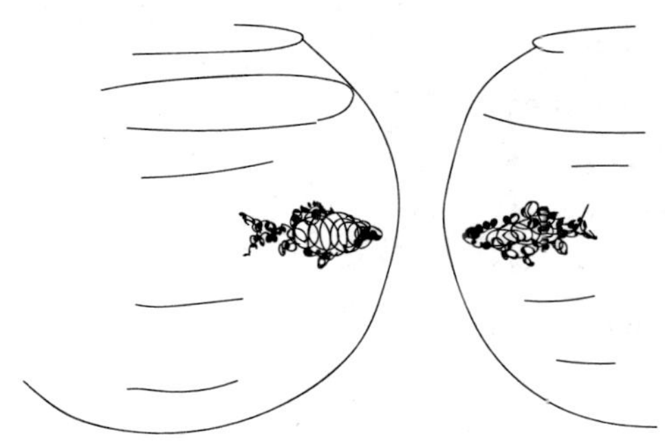

Our sleeping bed is our grave

After contemplating
on nothing
for hours and hours every night,
when I finally lie down
on my bed to sleep,
I feel as if
I am lying down in my own grave.

I persistently strive
to close my eyes
in order to escape my own being;
to merge myself
with the real/illusory world.

There is not much disparity
between the real world
and the illusory world,
between the death bell
and the incessant sleep;
either everything exists
or nothing exists.

When one sleeps
for a considerable number of hours,
one obtains considerable hours of life
from it
and when one sleeps
to never wake up again,
one obtains a new life with a new body
from it.

Our sleeping bed is our grave
and our dreams entail our changing epitaphs.

We have no control
over selecting our epitaphs,
as when the dream ends,
the sleeping bed becomes our grave
and the epitaphs themselves manifest
on our deceased faces.

Sensuality

Sensuality is ingrained
in the very nature of things
and pleasure is the only derivative
of all human endeavours.

There is no pleasure
superior to the pleasure
derived by the body
when it burns itself
on the pyre -
by willingly cooperating
with the fire.

There is no pleasure
superior to the pleasure
derived by the soul
when the material body
disintegrates into
independent constituent units
from its former
complex material state.

There is no pleasure
superior to the pleasure
derived by the mind
when the mind knows
that consciousness
is the by-product of matter.

Tomorrow never comes

Each day
each morning
starts with a promise.

A promise
that I will wake up
early in the morning
and exercise
from tomorrow onwards.

A promise
that I will only eat healthy food
and abstain
from drinking and smoking
from tomorrow onwards.

A promise
that I will not just survive
but I will live
a more meaningful life
from tomorrow onwards.

A promise
that I will never let down
my parents, beloved
and friends
from tomorrow onwards.

But each day
each evening
ends with guilt.

Guilt
that I could not wake up
early in the morning
and even skipped
my healthy meals
in exchange of
some unhygienic crap.

Guilt
that I find myself
sitting in a bar again;
drinking and smoking
to my heart's content.

Guilt
that I am just surviving
without a meaning
and purpose in my life.

Guilt
that my parents, beloved,
and friends
are all annoyed with me.

Tomorrow never comes
and each promise
turns into a guilt
in a matter of no time.

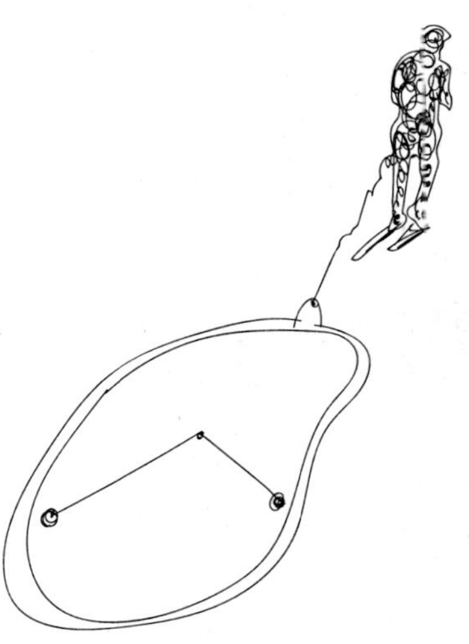

We all die in sin

What is held up against me
today,
can be held up against you
tomorrow.

We are all born in innocence
and we all die in sin,
not knowing exactly
what each of those words mean.

Intrinsically,
we human beings
are neither all good
nor all bad
but there seems to be
some indelible imprints
on the slates of our individual consciousness
that makes us feel
what we feel
and do
what we do
in a given situation.

Human beings
should never take credit
for all the so-called 'good' acts
that they partake in
unintentionally.

Human beings
should never blame
for all the so-called 'bad' acts
that they partake in
intentionally.

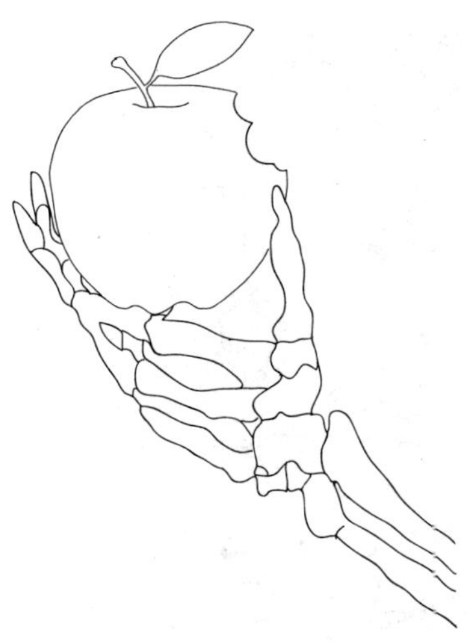

Nothing helps!

Neither learning
nor unlearning
helps.

What helps
is the understanding
that nothing helps.

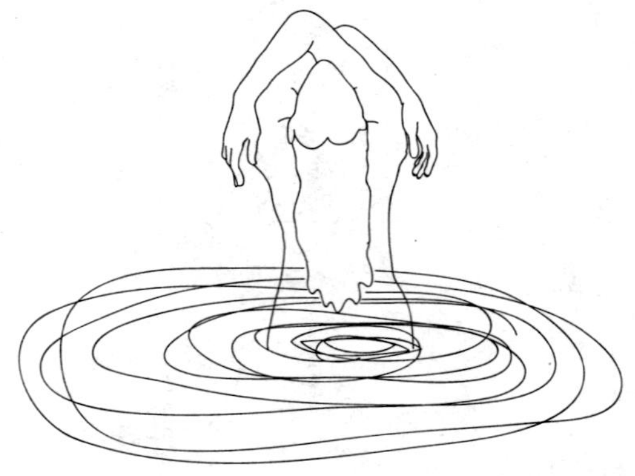

The other world

One after the other,
people are disappearing
from this world
to the so-called 'other world'.

Watching them depart,
makes me feel that maybe
this is not the first time
that I have been on this Earth.

My awareness
forces me to sense
that I have been on this Earth
many times before
and in whichever form
I had visited the Earth before,
I had always felt the same way
as I feel now – awestruck!

To lift the cloak of mystery
from the enigma of life and death,
I do not know
how many more births
I will have to take.

In this life,
I think it won't be possible
and I too
will have to disappear
while carrying
my wonderstruck eyes with me.

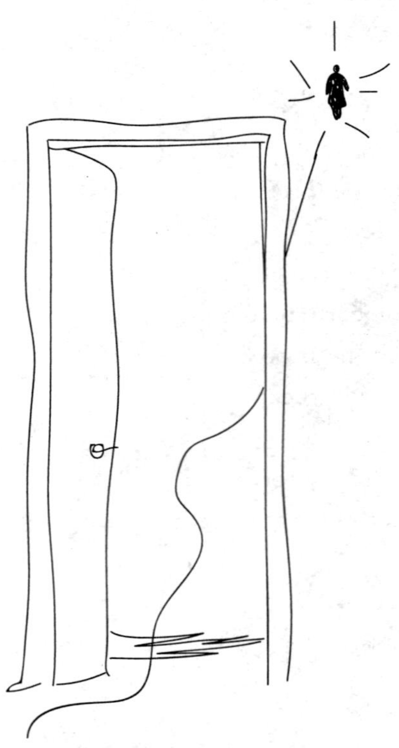

God is the real scarecrow

The scarecrows
positioned by humans
in the field
to scare the birds
from destroying the crops
are second-hand scarecrows.

After a while,
the birds get familiar
with the man-made structures
of scarecrows
and they shit on their head
while enjoying the food.

After all,
man-made scarecrows
are man-made scarecrows!

The real scarecrow is God
who neither discourages
nor encourages
the actions of any living entity.

Instead,
he gives all living entities
the mask of free-will
to choose their own actions,
which eventually guide
their individual destinies.

Seeds that couldn't blossom

The seeds
that couldn't blossom
into a flower
are the real seeds
for the ones
that blossomed
into a flower,
they withered away
and died
but the ones
that couldn't blossom
into a flower,
they resided in me
for a lifetime -
only to perish
at the time
of my death
in order to resurrect
and blossom again
in a different body,
in a different time,
and at a different place.

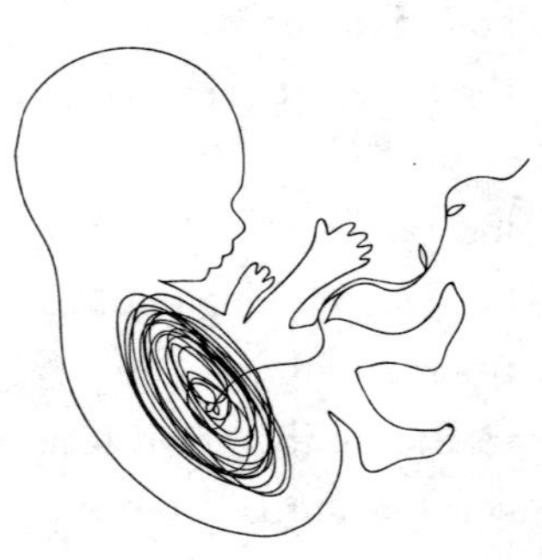

A perfidious lover street

There was a lane
and whenever
I used to pass by that lane,
all the dogs of that lane
would bark at me
in my disregard.

They didn't want me
in that lane
and they treated me
even worse than a monkey.

One of the reasons
for such despicable behaviour
was that
unlike in other lanes,
the male monkeys of that lane
would always gather
in large groups
to my rescue.

Dogs although
are considered most loyal
but the lane in discussion
was the lane of my beloved
and like my beloved,
the bitches of that lane
were also disloyal.

As far as the male monkeys
were concerned,
they too were oppressed
by the female monkeys
of that lane.

That lane
was later named -
'a perfidious lover street'.

The black chair

The black chair
in front of me
is vacant
at the moment.

It talks to me
more than a human ever could
when it is occupied.

It tells me
how redundant and frivolous
human talks are.

It tells me
how each word
that comes out of a human mouth
with its own distinct texture and sound
is a vain attempt to comprehend
the duality of life.

It tells me
how humans lie
while looking into
each other's eyes.

It tells me
how ecstatic
a vacant chair feels -
unburdened
by the weight of the human body
and thoughts.

I,
in my free time,
often sit on the floor
and look at the vacant chair
for hours
and it smiles back at me
sometimes.

Weekends

On weekends,
most people desire
to go out for a movie,
to eat in a fancy restaurant,
to shop,
or to go out on a two-day vacation.

On the other hand,
whenever I get a free day,
I prefer to go to the cremation ground
in order to understand this life
a little better.

I see people weeping
for the loss of their loved one.

I see a self-proclaimed priest
disinterestedly putting up the pyre
and chanting the mantras.

I see how boorishly
all the processions are carried out.

Once the dead person
is paid the last respect,
the pyre is put to fire
and all the five elements
the body is made up of
are set ablaze in it.

The tears slowly stop
and the mourners go home,
while I sit with the pyre -
gazing at it steadily
for the next ten to twelve hours,
till the fire converts the body
into ashes.

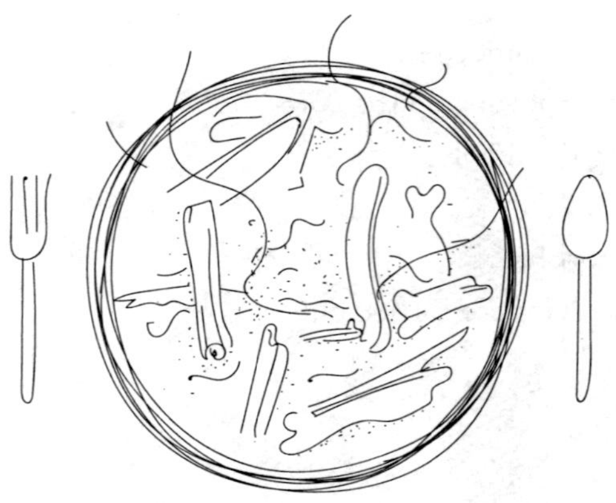

Death is my only beloved

Death is my only beloved,
as only death can fulfil
the yearning of my life.

Death is my only beloved
as only death can kill me
and make me immortal.

Death is my only beloved
as only death waits anxiously
for my death.

Death is my only beloved
as only death deserves
to love me,
for only she knows
my worth.

Death is my only beloved
as we are not two but one;
I am all life
and she is all death.

Death is my only beloved
for when life merges in death,
then only death remains -
my real true beloved.

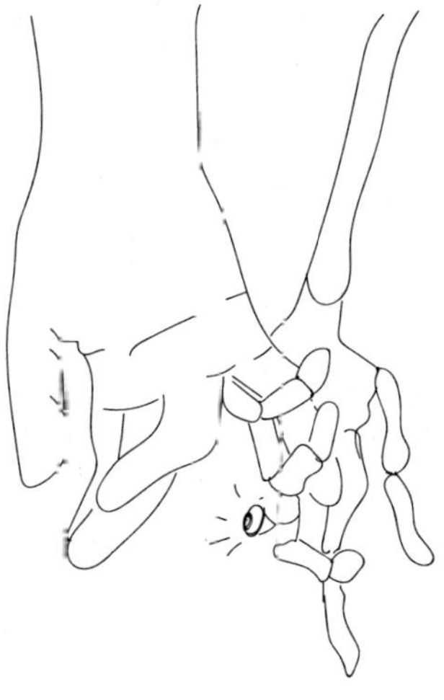

Live like strangers

Marry the one
whom you don't love
and marry the one
who doesn't love you.

Relationships among strangers
tend to last longer
as they know exactly
what they want from each other
and they get it
without any emotional bondage
arising out of some lame irrational promise
made in a nebulous moment.

Are you among those
who think that marriage
without feelings for someone
is not worth?

Well, here is a thought!

How many of us
actually end up
marrying the person
we love
or assumed we loved?

Marriage and love
are two totally different things.

Marriage is not a derivative of love
and love
is not a derivative of marriage,
although they can be
a derivative of each other
in some cases,
but only as an exception.

Probably,
if life gave us a chance
to die peacefully
on a comfortable bed
with an active consciousness,
then,
probably then
we would possibly get a clue
of whom we actually loved
in our respective lives.

Till then,
fuck like wild animals
and live like strangers.

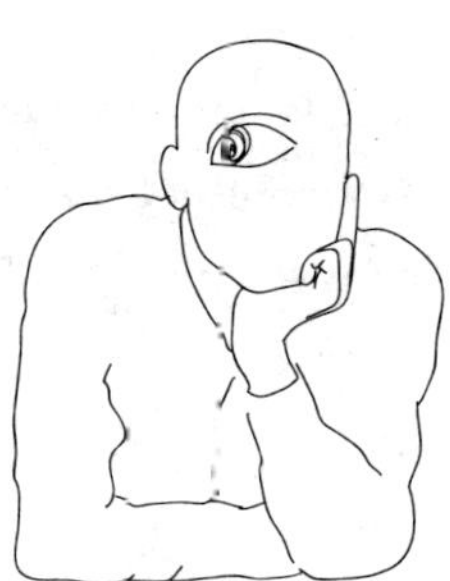

How are you?

Even if you consider it to be
a customary conversation starter,
never ask a poet
'how are you?'

The 'how' implies
that there ought to be
an answer to such a question.

The 'how' binds a poet
to pick an answer
from the many recognizable states
of mood and existence,
i.e. happy, sad, angry, etc. -
knowing very well
that no reply would be befitting
to such an appalling question.

A genuine poet
is a specimen of paradoxes;
thus, a poet is
simple yet complex,
innocent yet mature,
gentle yet wild,
happy yet sad,
and angry yet compassionate.

A poet feels
a plethora of emotions
each moment
without any fixed categorization
of pain and pleasure.

A poet never thinks
in terms of 'how'
and once
somebody puts that question,
a poet
by the very nature
of the interpreting mechanism
begins to think about 'how'.

The thinking
borne out of thoughts
never arrives
at a fixed legitimate answer
and it confuses a poet,
wherein a poet
is suddenly reminded
of a state in which
a person deliberately laughs
in order to cry
and deliberately cries
in order to laugh.

My kind of love

I have known and desired
only one kind of love.

A kind of love
in which a person
completely surrenders
his/her being
to the other person -
out of free will,
out of virtue,
and not out of weakness.

A kind of love
in which the ego
ebbs like smoke;
the 'I' disappears,
the 'you' disappears,
and only love remains.

A kind of love
in which the dichotomy
between life and death
dissolves;
in which a person
lives and dies
each moment.

A kind of love
in which there is no past
(the yesterdays),
and there is no future
(the tomorrows),
but only the present
(the here and now).

But some people
might even go to the extent
of calling such a kind of love
as blasphemous and utopian.

Tell me
who will be interested
in such a kind of love?

Who would want to surrender
such a delicate pearl-like heart
oozing with love and blood
to get butchered mercilessly
at the hands of another person
who has known and desired
a different kind of love.

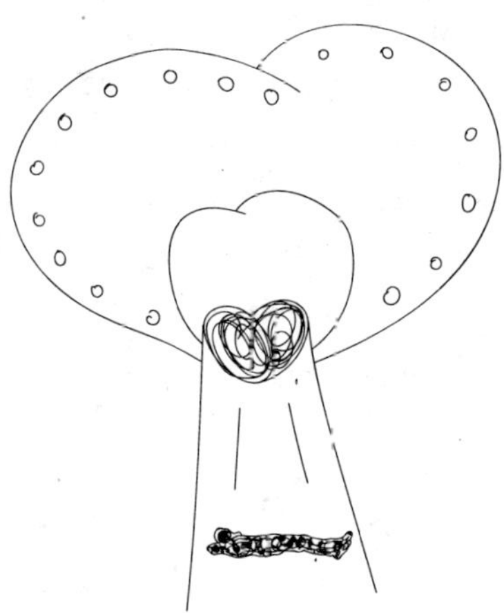

The only difference

The only difference
between you and me
is that you
will be buried
and I
will be cremated
after our respective deaths.

Our physical bodies
will fade away and merge
with the five basic elements -
leaving the souls aloof,
in a place where the Earth
and the sky meet.

Your soul
will again take a form
if there is still desire in you
but your search won't end.

Glimpse the unmanifest
in the manifest
and the manifest
in the unmanifest.

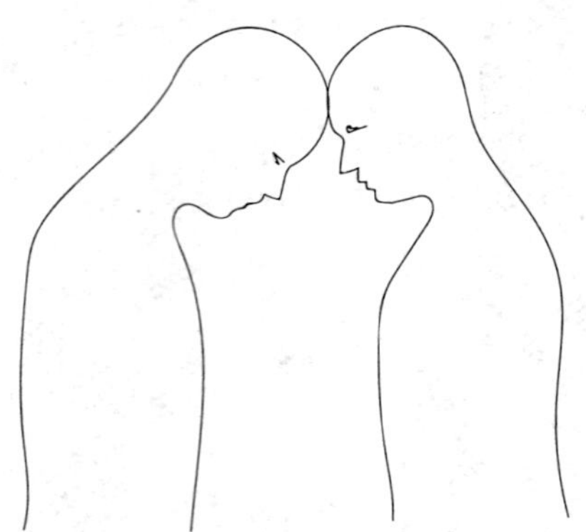

I am no Jesus

My life belongs
to all of you -
make use of it
while you still can.

There is no aim
or purpose
to my life
other than
being accessible
to you all
in my entirety.

I am no Jesus
but consider my flesh
your food
and my blood
your wine;
inhale
and exhale me
till I dissolve
in each one of you
completely.

My poetry is not a death song

My poetry
doesn't dissect life
with the eye of a scientist
who scrutinize pieces of existence
under a microscope
in the laboratory -
basing the arguments on past experiments
which might explain to some extent
how things work in a particular way
but can never explain
why things work in that particular way.

My poetry
doesn't dissect life
with the eye of a philosopher
who attempts to comprehend existence
with the help of known philosophies
that are all based on a premise
and are bound to fall flat anyhow
if one questions the premise
in the first place.

My poetry
doesn't dissect life
with the eye of a saint
who assumes that this whole existence
is brought into being
solely for the pleasure of mankind
and that we are all
at the centre of this existence,
whether we believe it or not.

My poetry
tries to appreciate and observe life
with the eye of a poet
who is lost in the wisdom of existence,
who is indifferent to both fact and fiction,
and who receives all answers,
even of those questions
which were never asked before.

My poetry
tries to appreciate and observe life
with the eye of a painter
who wishes to imitate and copy
the entire existence
on a sheet of paper
as closely as possible,
and who
in an attempt to accomplish it
always ends up adding
something more original
to the available knowable existence.

My poetry
understands and observes life
with the eye of a musician
who composes and sings
throughout life
just to touch those few
unheard and unfelt melodies;
the highs and lows in nature
with intrinsic nuances
of its own.

My poetry
originates from the known,
progresses towards the unknown,
and settles somewhere between
the known and the unknown.

My poetry
is not an obituary
of life
but a renaissance
of wonder.

Sinner

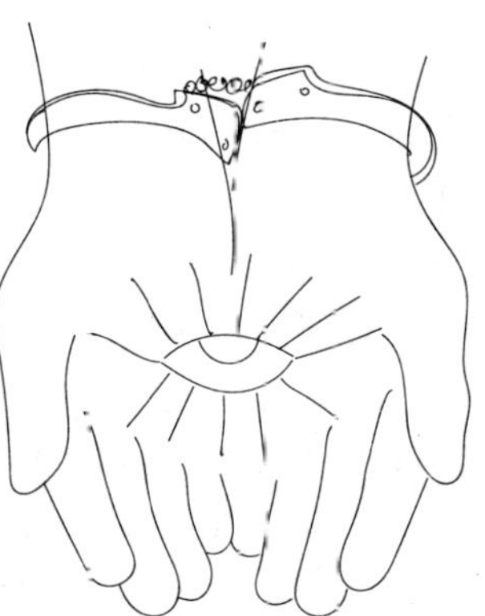

Do not forgive me, God,
for I have sinned.

Show me your omnipotence
by punishing me
to the best of your capabilities.

Show me your omniscience
by proving me guilty
and misconstruing my past,
present,
and future state of affairs.

Show me your omnipresence
by becoming my plaintiff's witness
in the court of law.

Show me your benevolence
by writing my death sentence
in front of your chosen people.

Show me your mercy
by offering me
a one-way ticket to hell -
the place I have admired
and always wanted to explore
after passing considerable years
on this Earth.

Alcohol and cigarettes

No matter
how much damage
alcohol and cigarettes
have caused to my health
but I still revere them
in the highest spirit.

Alcohol and cigarettes
helped me during heartbreaks,
depression, and anxiety attacks.

It helped me
in overcoming guilt, regrets,
and post-trauma emotions.

Although
other substances also helped me
in relieving the pain
but they only aided me
for a short period of time.

It was only alcohol and cigarettes
that stayed with me
and helped me in staying
the kind of person 'I am'
and not the kind of person
others want me 'to be'.

All in all,
alcohol and cigarettes
helped me survive
stitch by stitch,
without which
I would have committed suicide
long ago.

How inglorious it is
to survive
even after knowing
that there is no purpose
or meaning to any of this
and that all of this
will come to an end
someday,
better sooner than later.

Until I die

How many more mornings
will I have to wake up?

How many more afternoons
will I have to work?

How many more evenings
will I have to spend in the bar?

How many more nights
will I have to spend
in the company of the moon?

How many more years
will I have to survive like this
– drinking, smoking, whoring,
eating and shitting?

How many more months
will I have to
burn in the scorching heat,
freeze in the dead cold,
desiccate in the dry wind
and drench in rainy tears?

How many more days
will I have to breathe
and write poetry?

How many more hours
will I have to blabber
inconsistently?

How many more minutes
will I have to be
extremely silent?

How many more seconds
will I have to wait
until I die?

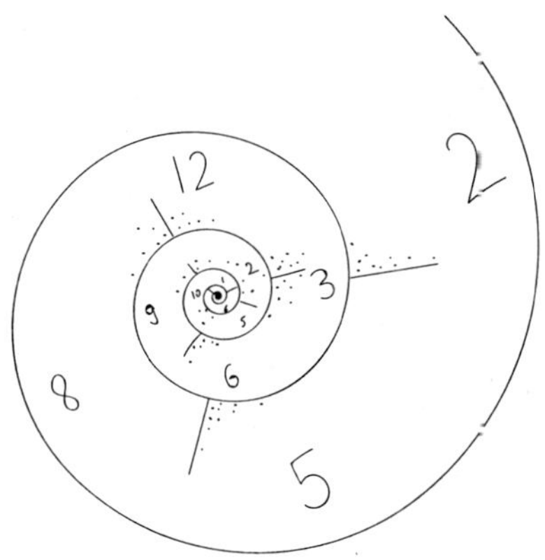

Solitude

Who are you?
I do not know.

Where did you come from?
Somewhere...

Where are you heading to?
Somewhere...

Why are you naked?
My flesh is my clothing.

Are you thirsty?
Probably!

Are you hungry?
Perhaps!

Where do you stay?
Nowhere...

Where can I find you again?
Everywhere...

Are you mad?
No.

What do you remember?
Nothing...

Do you want me to help you?
Maybe!

How?
Just leave me alone.

Can you take it?

I never see things
with your eyes.

I never hear things
with your ears.

I never smell things
with your nose.

I never taste things
with your tongue.

I never touch things
with your body.

I see, hear, smell,
taste and touch things
with my own eyes,
ears, nose, tongue,
and body -
that is what makes it
all the more different;
something which is not a part
of your experiencing structure.

I can offer you
my eyes, ears, nose,
tongue and body
to experience that
which you have been missing out
but the question is -
can you take it?

Remember

I didn't love you
how Romeo loved Juliet,
how Ranjha loved Heer,
how Majnu loved Laila,
how Mahiwal loved Soni,
how Salim loved Anarkali,
how Shah Jahan loved Mumtaz,
how Antony loved Cleopatra,
how Paris loved Helen,
how Abelard loved Heloise,
how Orpheus loved Eurydice,
how Keats loved Fanny Brawn,
how Yeats loved Maud Gonne,
how Dante loved Beatrice,
how Jaun Elia loved Fareha,
how Akhtar Sheerani loved Salma,
how Sartre loved Simone de Beauvoir,
how Heidegger loved Arendt,
how Shakespeare loved Lucy Negro,
how Fitzgerald loved Zelda Sayre,
how Baudelaire loved Jeanne Duval,
and how many more like them loved
many others like them.

I loved you
how I (Laudeep) loved you
and I want you
to remember that
in whatever way possible
as per your convenience.

Be courageous

We all have to leave
this world
someday or the other,
so why cry
that somebody left early?

So what if an infant
never reached teenage?

So what if a teenager
never reached adulthood?

So what if an adult
never reached old age?

So what if an oldie
never reached 100?

Life is one colossal warehouse
of good and bad experiences
gathered right from the moment
of birth
to the moment of death
and we all know
that more bad experiences are piled up
in the collective memory of humankind
in comparison to the good experiences.

To die early
by natural or unnatural means
is a blessing on this Earth
for those
who are not courageous enough
to commit suicide.

I drink to exist

I never had a drink in my life
for the sake of pleasure,
for the sake of leisure,
for the sake of merriment,
for the sake of love,
for the sake of friendship,
for the sake of compassion,
for the sake of gratitude,
for the sake of
numbing my sense organs,
for the sake of
having better conversations,
or for the sake of peace,
contentment, beatitude and bliss.

I always had a drink in my life
to simply exist,
to simply survive,
to simply be myself,
and to simply make sense
of my reality as it is
without knowing what it is.

Consciousness

I require
only that much consciousness
which helps me
to observe,
experience,
think,
and write.

Any sudden flare-up
of consciousness
more than I require
makes me want to puke
my guts out.

There is no art of living

There is no art of living,
as the art of living entails
that there is a certain way,
a certain manner in which
human beings should live,
behave, think, feel, and react.

The art of living focuses
on the unambiguous,
thus rejecting everything
that doesn't fall
within the fence of
the so-called 'goodness'.

The art of living misses
the totality of life
which includes all the 'vices'
and without the totality of life,
life is just a series
of unexamined events -
one frame after another.

I can give away my life
for a single moment of mergence
with the totality of life
that embraces vices as dearly
as it embraces the good,
rather than live for eternity
with a fraction of life
subject to 'goodness'.

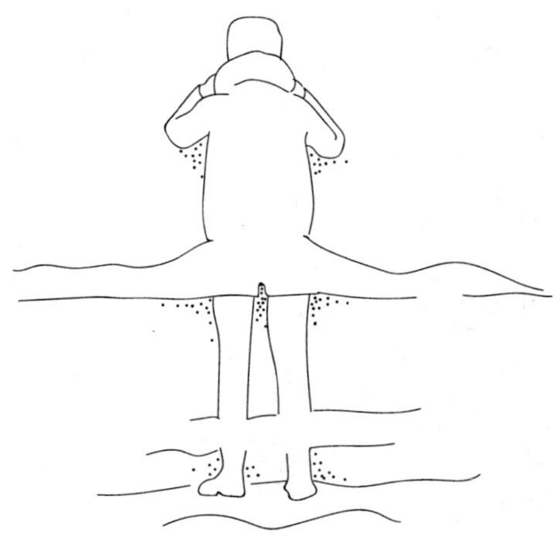

Incarcerate

I like to capture
dead things in my camera
to contrast them
with the vitality of life
by the power of my vision.

In the past week only
I captured a fallen tree,
a plucked flower,
a stagnant river,
a broken mountain,
a destroyed nest
and a stillborn baby.

Then I took out a canvas
and started to sketch
while gazing
at the captured photos.

First I drew
a broken mountain
in the background.

Then I drew
a stagnant river
surrounding the broken mountain
on all sides.

Then I drew
a fallen tree
in the stagnant river.

Then I drew
a destroyed nest
on the branch of the fallen tree.

Then finally I drew
a stillborn baby
lying in the destroyed nest
with a plucked flower in hand.

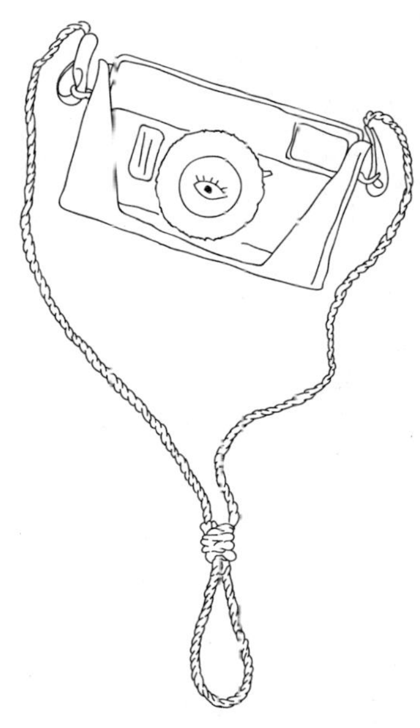